Building a *World-Class* Financial Services Business

How to Transform Your Sales Practice into a Company Worth Millions

DON SCHREIBER, JR.

DEARBORN™
TRADE
A **Kaplan Professional** Company

Vice President and Publisher: Cynthia A. Zigmund
Editorial Director: Donald J. Hull
Senior Project Editor: Trey Thoelcke
Interior Design: Lucy Jenkins
Cover Design: Design Solutions
Cover Illustration: Astrid Dininno/SIS
Typesetting: the dotted i

Published by Dearborn Trade, a Kaplan Professional Company

Printed in the United States of America

01   02   03   10   9   8   7   6   5   4   3   2   1

Library of Congress Cataloging-in-Publication Data

Schreiber, Don.
    Building a world-class financial services business / Don Schreiber.
        p.   cm.
    Includes index.
    ISBN 0-7931-4490-6 (6x9 hdbk)
    1. Financial planners. 2. Investment advisors. 3. Financial services industry. I. Title.
    HG179.5 .S37 2001
    332.6′068—dc21

                                        2001001204

I dedicate this book to my wife, Holly, and my children, Matt and Ann, who allowed me to make an investment of our time together to complete this project. They are truly my best friends.

I want to thank my dad, who in sharing his daily trials and travails about building his business taught me the wisdom of global problem solving and the need for a written strategic plan.

Thanks to all of the staff of Wealth Builders for sharing the vision; with special thanks to Bob Confessore, Gary Stroik, and Tom Duffy for not only sharing the vision, but for implementing the plan.

Great thanks to Larry Chambers, writing coach and editor, for his help in planning and developing this book. He made a difficult and overwhelming process seem truly manageable.

C O N T E N T S

INTRODUCTION

The Big Question

Are You Building a Sales Practice or a Business?

You are probably aware of the current trend in the financial services industry of broker-dealer groups going around the country offering to buy financial planning and advisory practices. Sadly, many planners and advisors are discovering that their businesses have little, if any, equity value. They may be very successful and even generate a substantial personal income, but the revenue they create is dependent on their continuing to work the business every day. This presents a major challenge: How can a financial planning professional maximize his or her current income (sales) and still build a business (equity) that can be sold at a later date? To many planners, these goals appear to be diametrically opposed.

My name is Don Schreiber, Jr. I am CEO and President of Wealth Builders, Inc., an independent asset management and planning firm located in Little Silver, New Jersey. My colleagues and I have built this successful business, which has grown from less than $100,000 in annual revenue with no equity to more than $2 million in annual revenue and over $118 million dollars of assets under management. It is a business that we could sell for $8 to $10 million—that is, if we wanted to sell it.

Would you be able to sell your practice for what you think it's worth? Most financial advisors who answer honestly would have to say *no*. That's not because they haven't worked hard to develop their practices or because they aren't successful. Many advisors we talked to have built practices that earn well over $1 million a year, but have little inherent equity; plus, they say they aren't netting as much personal income as they should. A recent compensation study sponsored by the Financial Planning Association (FPA) reported that the average sole practitioner financial planner makes only about $95,000 annually. The painful truth is they really don't own businesses, they "own" jobs. And you can't sell a job!

If you'd like to hear the other side of the story and learn what you can do to turn your successful practice into a valuable business while increasing your net income—read on. If you have always been commission based and want to convert to recurring fee revenue, this book is the road map you've been looking for. Also, for those of you just starting out in the financial planning arena, we will show you a successful business model.

This book will show you how to offer the best available planning and investment advice to your clients and, at the same time, provide them with the highest level of ongoing service. I'm talking about levels of advice and service that are difficult—if not impossible—for your competitors to duplicate and that will help you create significant equity in your business. That, in a nutshell, is the ultimate opportunity in today's marketplace for financial planners and investment advisors.

Two dynamic areas of change that are rewriting the rules of the game are an *influx of capital* and *revolutionary changes in technology*. The most important and potentially devastating is the influx of investing capital from financial conglomerates. Because of the tremendous growth in affluence in the United States over the past decade, corporate America is targeting the financial services business as the high-profit sector of the future. They see the affluent investor as the key to significant long-term profit and growth. In other words, everyone has their eyes on your clients.

Commissions Are Heading toward Zero

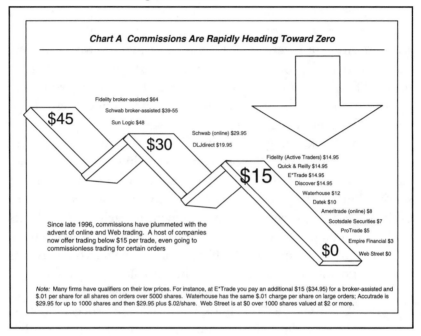

Chart A Commissions Are Rapidly Heading Toward Zero

$45

$30

$15

$0

Fidelity broker-assisted $64
Schwab broker-assisted $39-55
Sun Logic $48

Schwab (online) $29.95
DLJdirect $19.95

Fidelity (Active Traders) $14.95
Quick & Reilly $14.95
E*Trade $14.95
Discover $14.95
Waterhouse $12
Datek $10
Ameritrade (online) $8
Scotsdale Securities $7
ProTrade $5
Empire Financial $3
Web Street $0

Since late 1996, commissions have plummeted with the advent of online and Web trading. A host of companies now offer trading below $15 per trade, even going to commissionless trading for certain orders

Note: Many firms have qualifiers on their low prices. For instance, at E*Trade you pay an additional $15 ($34.95) for a broker-assisted and $.01 per share for all shares on orders over 5000 shares. Waterhouse has the same $.01 charge per share on large orders; Accutrade is $29.95 for up to 1000 shares and then $29.95 plus $.02/share. Web Street is at $0 over 1000 shares valued at $2 or more.

To make matters worse, advances in technology continue to shrink profits as well as eliminate many services that do not add significant value to your clients. A great example is electronic trading over the Internet. Trading, once a profit center and mainstay service of Wall Street brokerage firms, is being offered directly to investors over the Internet, and the cost of buying financial products is approaching zero.

Now for some good news. Today's Wall Street executives and stockbrokers are trying to develop a business model that looks a lot like ours, the independent planner/investment advisor model based on providing affluent clients with turnkey financial advice and management for a fee. As these well-capitalized competitors use their marketing muscle, operational strength, and ability to harness technology, they will be able to entice your clients with solutions that are cheaper and faster than anything you can offer.

What they don't understand, though, is that affluent investors not only want turnkey financial advice and management, but *also a trusted relationship with an individual who is a knowledgeable professional.* Affluent investors seek to align themselves with someone they can trust to provide these services across all areas of their financial life. *The good news is that you already know how to provide affluent investors with what they want*—something these large competitors cannot yet deliver!

In this book, I'm going to show you how to develop a strategic business model that exploits your competitive advantage to secure trusted, personal relationships, allowing you not only to survive, but also to prosper. It will enable you to deliver the highest quality advice, service, and management to each of your clients while continuing to grow your business. A written strategic business plan that encompasses the big picture of where your business needs to go will become a guide to how to align your company's resources in your day-to-day operations to get there.

I'd like to say that this book will make the process painless, but it won't. Although it is structured as a comprehensive, step-by-step strategic business model program, you will have to make the commitment to follow the program and begin to manage by design, rather than operating your company by the seat of your pants. You will acquire the tools to help you define your company mission, determine your strategic objectives, prioritize your goals, outline a timeline, and plot milestones to measure your progress and keep on track. Most importantly, you will learn how to avoid the mistakes many independent financial planning firms are still making.

Where did I get this knowledge? I was lucky; I had a great teacher. Over the years developing his own business, my dad explained to me that being a business owner was really about problem solving: not just the day-to-day problems, but the big-picture problems of how to grow, how to earn a profit, and how to build equity. I learned the importance of strategic planning and the need to put that plan, covering every aspect of growing and managing the business, in writing. The strategic planning process is the hardest job I ever encountered, but it is also the most rewarding.

By following the strategic business planning prescription in this book, you can build a world-class financial services business, not just a sales practice. And it will be a business that provides clients with the highest levels of advice and service, provides your employees with rewarding career opportunities, and provides you with the opportunity to become an industry leader and to build equity in your business beyond your wildest expectations.

From a Job You Hate to a Business You'll Love

1

Why Financial Advisors Play the Loser's Game

There's a good reason why well-meaning, hard-working advisors and planners find themselves with an all-consuming *job* and very little or no equity in their practices. Most have copied the methods and structures of their seemingly successful mentors rather than creating a written, detailed strategic business plan designed specifically to meet their own objectives. Following the way things have been done in the past will result in the same outcome.

So before you begin redesigning your practice into a business, let's examine the most common, and most debilitating, mistakes we as *owners* of a financial planning practice or investment advisory business often make.

Mistake #1. We channel all of our clients' service and advice through one person. As a result, the clients see little value in the rest of our organization.

In our business model, no one person is responsible for providing advice, ongoing service, and relationship management to clients. Our goal is to maintain a relationship with all of the clients who have helped us build our business over the years. We want to provide them with an outstanding level of service, turning them into our best referral advocates. We do this by leveraging technology, institutionalizing our service delivery process, and hiring and training people to provide a level of advice and service almost impossible for our competitors to duplicate.

By following this business model, you will be able to build equity in your business. At the same time, your life will become more manageable, because it will be your *business* that is providing clients with the services they need and want, not *you*.

Mistake #2. We focus on gross revenue, not recurring revenue.

When we discovered that our gross income meant very little in terms of building equity, we started to focus on building a business that had recurring revenue. These revenue streams provide a more predictable cash flow, which allows us to plan for business expansion and profitability. When we focused on building recurring revenue, we found that we could increase our personal income with a more predictable net profit.

Remember: The prime determinant of equity value is your level of sustainable profitability.

Mistake #3. We eat what we kill.

I call this the hunter/gatherer syndrome. When I started in the industry as an independent financial planner, I focused almost exclusively on my payout—if I could get an 85 percent payout, that was great. If I could get 95 percent, that was better. And if a broker-dealer would pay me 105 percent of my commissions, that was ideal. Little, if any, money went back into the business; I spent everything I made—no matter how much that was.

Many of us in the financial services profession have learned to gorge ourselves: big houses, sports cars, boats—whatever the trend of a particular year, we have to have it. *Earn high current income and spend it* has been the business model for many of us in the financial planner/broker community. This out-of-date model permeates most of our industry and may continue as the single biggest struggle many of us face. Building a business requires significant reinvestment of capital, but many planners take 60 to 80 percent of each sales dollar out of the practice as compensation. Most successful service companies have a direct sales cost of between 20 and 50 percent. To build equity, we need to pour some of our income back into the business.

This syndrome has also created an entire industry of *salespeople* with a survivalist attitude that prevents them from being compensated for the effort and risk required of a *business owner.*

Mistake #4. Our personal vision doesn't match our corporate objective.

Whatever our personal objectives are, we need to make sure that our business is aligned to accomplish them. Many financial planners have shared with me that, at the end of the week, they feel personally bankrupt. They often find they are unable to participate with their family or pursue personal interests because they feel emotionally and physically drained. All too often, any personal needs wait until the demand of the business is satisfied, which is seldom possible. If your business is going to facilitate your personal objectives, you must first determine what your personal life and financial goals truly are.

Mistake #5. We fail to diversify our asset bases away from our businesses.

Just as the line between our personal and business goals is not always clearly drawn, the boundary between our personal and our business finances may be a bit hazy, too.

If you are going to build a successful business, you must take the risk of owning the business away from your personal finances. You must diversify your asset base and learn how to retain capital, because a business without capital of its own requires you to take money out of your own pocket. If a shortfall occurs, you have to cover it. No wonder you feel so strongly about retaining control over the business.

Mistake #6. We don't really know who or how big our target market is.

In order to develop an effective financial planning practice, you must know who your ideal clients are and what they want. Here are some statistics for you to consider:

- Thirty-five million Americans are age 65 or older, and they're the wealthiest generation the world has ever seen. Seniors represent $14 trillion in investable assets.
- Three million small businesses will pass from one generation to the next over the next five years. Small business owners in the United States represent the most affluent target market. They have more complex financial situations than non-business owners and, therefore, require the most help. This market segment is comprised primarily of delegators: people who are looking for a trustworthy, knowledgeable financial advisor to provide them with turnkey financial advice and management—someone whom they can trust and rely on to be their financial quarterback. They are not particularly price sensitive and are willing to pay for top-quality advice.
- Seventy-seven million baby boomers represent $4 trillion, mostly invested in retirement plans. For the most part, the baby boomers are doing quite well financially and are just entering their peak savings years.
- Fifty million Generation Xers, people who are under 31 years old, mostly have not begun to accumulate savings or investment assets.

Which of these groups is your target market? For us, the target market is obvious. Seniors are, on average, the most affluent. They own many of the small businesses that require complex problem solving, and they are willing to delegate and pay for the advice and service they desire. Plus, the market is huge: only about 20,000 financial planners provide comprehensive planning—potentially 1,750 senior clients for each financial planner.

Mistake #7. We offer the wrong product or service.

"Get rich quick!" That attitude permeates our society and is a cancer in our business culture. Many winning business models fail because the owner doesn't stick with the plan. To become successful, we need to develop our business plan fully and adhere to it, not abandon it for the newest fad or idea that we think will make us rich.

For example, over the past five years, many of the industry's most successful investment advisors (formerly financial planners) have been telling anyone who will listen that we should be offering investment advice for a fee. "Forget about financial planning," they say. "These services are too expensive and time consuming to deliver and are comprised of task sets that cannot be easily automated. Concentrate instead on gathering investment assets, building your assets under management."

We think this logic is faulty for two reasons. First, affluent investors want turnkey financial advice across all areas of their financial life. The financial planning industry has already won this particular war. Over the past 20 years, consumers have been educated to the considerable personal benefits available through personal financial planning. Our target customer wants comprehensive advice; they can get investment advice and management from anyone.

Second, a business model built only on investment advice and asset management is bound to falter when the markets revert to normal investment cycles, which include periods of negative performance. If returns are negative for six or eight quarters (normal market cycles) and you can only talk to clients about investment performance, you're going to lose a significant portion of your business. Also, because investment advice has become a commodity in recent years, pricing and pressure on profits are making asset management much less attractive as a stand-alone business model.

Mistake #8. We don't put our business plan in writing.

As stated above, many winning business models fail because the owner doesn't stick with a business plan. One of the main reasons is that the owner fails to put the plan in writing, thus creating a roadmap to success.

By drawing up a written business plan, we create a synthesis of our personal goals in our business. However, most of us are too busy putting out daily fires to do any planning. We do what is urgent, not necessarily what's important. We lose sight of the fact that we are in business to create the opportunity for a more satisfying life.

Strategic planning often takes a back seat unless time for it is scheduled. Even then, it is easily postponed—not because it's so difficult, but because most of us just don't know how to begin. Yet, we repeatedly perform this service for clients. When you think of planning as being a facilitator to achieve personal life goals, it becomes fun. When you document the process, others in your company can follow it. If you choose to carry your plan in your mind, you will have to be physically present all the time. None of your knowledge is transferable. More importantly, your operations cannot be systematically improved.

Mistake #9. We fail to clarify our partnering relationships.

If you're like most financial professionals, you've created referral relationships with CPAs, plan administrators, and lawyers. In the past, these professionals probably worked on an hourly basis with their clients and avoided giving investment advice. You educated them on the value of professional money management, and they were impressed by the value you added.

But today, many of these same professions will soon be creating their own registered advisory companies. In many cases, where the referring professional is the primary advisor with these clients, you may be out of luck.

On the other hand, if you formalize the relationship in writing, you won't be caught off guard. You may even be able to become the money management arm of their business. Clarify your partnering relationships. Take some time to assess the value you bring to the relationships. If you can't readily identify the value, your partners won't perceive it either.

Mistake #10. We fail to institutionalize our management practice.

The fundamental difference between having a business as opposed to a sales practice is institutionalizing the relationship between the clients and the business.

For a long time, I thought it was great when clients thought I was Mr. Wonderful. They depended on me to solve their problems, and I took those relationships very seriously. Then I realized that my attitude was really an inhibitor to building a business. The more clients I had, the more difficult it became for me to provide advice, service, and relationship management in the way I felt was necessary. I had to find a way to provide a level of advice and service to all clients as if I were giving it to them personally, but without taking that responsibility myself. This required putting systems in place so that when clients call, they feel they can work with anyone in the organization and get the same satisfaction. Institutionalizing makes the difference between having a job and building a business.

Mistake #11. We have no formal cash flow management system.

In any business, cash flow management is critical. By designing a financial management system to track income, expenses, and profit on a timely basis, we will make better financial and business decisions.

For example: Many practitioners price their planning service at the low end of the scale, almost giving away this service, in the hope of enticing clients into giving them their investment business. In essence, they are making the planning service a loss leader. One thing you learn quickly as you analyze your business—there is no such thing as a loss leader. Loss leaders are just money losers, and guess whose money you are losing? Yours.

Mistake #12. We fail to develop an exit strategy.

Most of us have no exit strategy, but in reality we should be prepared from day one. The same ingredients that will be attractive to a buyer someday will also make our businesses run more smoothly while we're building them.

If your business depends on your presence, you may not have any equity to sell. Even if you can find a buyer, you may be required to become an employee of the new owner for three to five years. Plan your exit strategy accordingly.

Also, spend some quality time on your financial statements and pro forma estimates, because many strategic buyers will want to pay you based on your delivering your numbers.

Next, let's take a look at how these mistakes undermine the financial planning practice and keep you from building equity in your business.

2

The Advisor Who
Can Sell Anything
but the Business

A few years ago, while conducting a mentoring meeting with a group of senior financial advisors about the concepts of recurring revenue and client retention, one of the participants, Jerry (not his real name), told us he had been talking to a consolidator who was looking to buy financial advisory practices.

Jerry wanted our help in figuring out how much his business was worth. When asked to name a value on his practice, he responded, "Conservatively, it's worth about $900,000." Jerry had been averaging around $300,000 in income a year, almost all of it generated from commissions. In other words, Jerry has to go out and create income every day; his business is completely dependent on his own efforts.

I didn't have the heart to tell him that his business wasn't worth anywhere near what he thought and that, in fact, he didn't even own a business—what he owned was a job.

Jerry told us the number of clients he has, their demographics, and how much he thought his "business" could grow. He proudly announced how many clients in his town depend on him— *mistake #1*. He explained how he had developed relationships with two large companies to provide retirement planning seminars and advice to downsized employees. These seminars were providing him with a steady stream of new IRA rollovers averaging approximately $300,000. He has been investing these rollovers in the same way for years in a combination of class A and B share mutual funds, creating diversified strategic portfolios.

Next Jerry told us he has $30 million invested in mutual funds, which generates a trail commission of 25 basis points (about $75,000 a year), plus he earns about $3,750 in planning fees and has a little over $60,000 from insurance business.

EXAMPLE 1   Jerry's Commission-Based Practice Overview

Existing Money Invested in Load Funds	$30,000,000
New Money Invested in Load Funds Annually	$4,000,000
Commissions on Load Funds	$160,000
Equity Trails	$75,000
Planning Fees	$3,750
Insurance Commissions	$30,000
Group Insurance Commissions	$15,000
Insurance Trails	$16,250
Total Revenue	$300,000

I turned to the group, ten of his peers, and posed the question to them: "How much would any of you pay for Jerry's business?" Heads were shaking back and forth, but no one said a word. Finally, one advisor broke the silence, saying, "I wouldn't pay anything for it." Then another said he might pay somewhere in the neighborhood of $50,000.

Jerry was shocked—in fact, he started to get a little angry. What he didn't understand is that commission-based businesses have little value to anyone other than the salesperson. Jerry's practice provides immediate gratification for sales, but delayed gratification for investing in his future. Many advisors are enjoying a decent, even affluent, life. Why should they cut back now for the promise of greater rewards tomorrow?

Planning and advisory practices are frequently evaluated and sold based on *cash flow*. By calculating net cash flow, the buyer can determine how much cash they get to keep after paying operating expenses and sales and manager costs. In Jerry's current situation, a simplified cash flow calculation will look like this:

EXAMPLE 2   Jerry's Fee-Based Practice Overview

Revenue	$300,000
– Sales and/or Owners Compensation*	150,000
= Gross Profit	150,000
– Overhead Expenses	120,000
= Cash Flow before Taxes	$ 30,000

*Reasonable sales compensation set at 50 percent of revenue

In the best case, if we ignore taxes, a motivated buyer might offer Jerry five to six times cash flow before tax, or $150,000 to $180,000, for his practice. When Jerry heard this, he threw up his hands and said he would just continue to work. He said he could make twice as much in one year. Like many of us, Jerry was missing the point—the only income source attractive to a buyer would be the equity trails his practice generated from recurring income; that is, not dependent on the new owner going out and repeating Jerry's sales effort.

No one is going to say that Jerry hasn't been doing a really good job. He has $30 million invested in load mutual funds, gets trails each year, has some planning fees, some group insurance, some life insurance—all the income sources one normally has as part of the financial planning practice. Our advice to him was to change the structure of his organization from a sales practice to a business, and change the focus of his revenue from up-front commissions to recurring revenue.

Recurring revenue streams are much more valuable than non-recurring revenue streams. This one small adjustment could alter

Jerry's picture dramatically. For instance, if he took the $30 million invested in mutual funds that generates a trail commission of 25 basis points ($75,000 a year) and put it under management at a one percent annual fee, he would bring in the same $300,000 a year but in *recurring* revenue. This would increase the value of his practice to about $580,000—almost a fourfold increase—because a buyer would pick up not merely commission trails, but rather a significant amount (about $300,000) of sustainable fee-based revenue.

EXAMPLE 3   Jerry's Fee-Based Practice Overview

Existing Assets Under Management	$30,000,000
New Money Placed Under Management	$4,000,000
Fees on Assets Under Management @ 1%	$300,000
Equity Trails	$0
Planning Fees	$3,750
Insurance Commissions	$30,000
Group Insurance Commissions	$15,000
Insurance Trails	$16,250
Total Revenue	$365,000

This time when the group was asked what anyone would pay for Jerry's practice, the responses ranged from one to three times recurring revenue: $300,000 to $900,000. That was obviously a much better outcome for Jerry, but I believe most people in the group were still missing the point: it doesn't matter what you do to the income structure of your practice if the relationship with the client remains the same. *Client and revenue retention will be a problem as long as the client perceives that the planner is the focal point of advice and service.* The transfer of client relationships from the individual to the organization is the critical factor in whether that income stream is really valuable. The group may have felt that Jerry's business was worth more if the $300,000 he earned each year came from recurring revenue, rather than commissions. However, from a buyer's perspective, the key is whether they can count on the revenue being there after they have purchased the practice and Jerry has walked away. Recurring revenue from fees is much more predictable and less dependent on new sales activity than commissions, but the most important factor is the transferability of the client relationship.

In a commission-based practice, client retention level is low. When a financial planning practice is sold, the average client retention is only about 15 percent. Think about that. More than three-quarters of a planner's clients leave the firm when he does.

By having his firm provide management of mutual fund assets and converting his compensation structure from commissions to fees, Jerry's practice could increase client retention levels from 15 percent to 50 percent or more. And that's basically where the business value changes significantly, because the firm is much more likely to keep that revenue rolling in.

Converting from commission to fees is a great first step to increasing your practice revenue and equity value. But it is only the first step. To truly unlock the maximum value and potential of your business, you must institutionalize your client relationships and your business model. By converting your sales practice to an institutional quality business, you empower your entire organization to deliver value-added advice and service to clients. Clients then perceive value in doing business with your company, regardless of whom they have as a planner. This change in perception helps ensure high client retention, which leads to predictable revenue retention—and predictable revenue supercharges your equity value.

If clients are completely dependent on one person in a financial planning practice, how likely are they to maintain a relationship with the firm if it's sold to someone else? Not very. In a situation like this, the business owner would probably have to spend a significant amount of time after the sale trying to transfer her client relationships to the new owner, often with little success. Clients have vested all of the perceived value in the departing planner; they see little reason to stay, so logically they look for a new planner.

The reason is easy to understand. To these clients, the planner *is* the practice. When we channel all of our client services and advice through one person—usually ourselves—the rest of our organization

Jerry's Valuation Model

Business Profile	Commission-Based Sales Practice	Fee-Based Sales Practice	Fee-Based Business
Existing Assets Invested in Load Funds	$30,000,000	$0	$0
New Money Invested in Load Product	$4,000,000	$0	$0
Existing Assets Under Fee Management	$0	$30,000,000	$30,000,000
New Assets Under Management	$0	$4,000,000	$4,000,000
Overhead Expense Factor	25.00%	25.00%	40.00%
Retention Assumptions			
Financial Planning Fees	25.00%	25.00%	85.00%
Equity Commissions	15.00%	15.00%	50.00%
Equity Trails	25.00%	25.00%	50.00%
Asset Management Fees	50.00%	50.00%	85.00%
Group Compensation	25.00%	25.00%	85.00%
Insurance Commission	0.00%	0.00%	25.00%
Value	$239,109	$584,981	$886,821

is perceived to have little value. Sure, clients may turn to a service person with a question regarding how to withdraw money or to have a statement explained. The fact is, though, clients attach little value to such details. When they want to discuss something important, they only want to talk to their financial planner. Indeed, we see many planners' clients experiencing a crisis of confidence when their planner is away on vacation.

John Bowen, a top consultant on acquisitions, recently told a seminar, "What buyers are really looking for is a business that is not dependent on the owner, where the owner can just walk away and the business would survive. But with most practices we see today, the advisor has to stay for five years after the firm is sold to make it viable."

What we are talking about is an institutional quality business. To create value in your practice, you must convert your practice into a business by institutionalizing your relationship with your clients, thus creating a business model that isn't wholly dependent on the advisor. You have to change the fundamental advisor/client relationship, shifting the focus away from yourself and onto your practice.

If you're like many successful financial advisors, you've probably overextended yourself. You've grown tired of being the only cog in the wheel. You've become overwhelmed, and you think the only way out may be to sell your practice. Many planners feel something like gratitude for acquisition groups—the way a rabbit might be grateful when the hunter comes along and pulls the trap from its leg. That image may not be the most flattering, but if you've found yourself ensnared in your practice, then you know it contains an element of truth.

There is an easier way. However, taking it will require a conscious effort on your part, and you are going to have to deal with a difficult issue: what I call *ego deflation*. Let's face it: most of us enjoy a bit of an ego rush by being responsible for another person's or family's entire financial future, and that's not easy to let go.

On the other hand, each of us who has been in this heady position understands that this level of responsibility and trust has a significant downside. We lose any opportunity for a quality personal life, and the more people we shove through this production vehicle, the worse our life gets.

This situation often leads advisors to cut their client base to make their working lives more manageable. Indeed, conventional wisdom from practice management consultants around the country is telling overwhelmed advisors to do just that. "Just throw away your small, less profitable clients," these consultants say, "and work with fewer large clients." Unfortunately, many planners are taking this suggestion to heart, because until now this seemed to be the only solution.

Advisors rationalize dropping clients because they feel overwhelmed, but this "solution" does not address the fundamental problem. Yes, they have fewer clients, but larger clients are much more demanding, requiring just as much, if not more, service than the small clients they let go. The fundamental problem is that you still have a sales practice, which channels all advice and service through one or two key people.

Let's review which of the common mistakes Jerry is making by following his current business model:

- *Mistake #1.* Jerry's model is based on Jerry's being the focal point of advice and service in his practice.
- *Mistake #2.* He has focused on generating high current gross revenue by using commission-based products to implement his planning recommendations.
- *Mistake #3.* Jerry spends most of the commissions he earns after paying for his office expenses to support a comfortable lifestyle. He is reluctant to build any infrastructure because he is the primary service provider and wants to keep expenses low by doing a lot of the work himself.
- *Mistake #4.* His idea of what his business is worth is very different than its actual value, and he continues to undermine his objective of building equity by pursuing his current method of operation.
- *Mistake #5.* Jerry's focus on current income prevents him from developing the model of ongoing advice and service that clients prefer. Commission-based models do not support the building of the business infrastructure required to provide continuity of advice and service to clients.

- *Mistake #6.* Jerry has not taken the time to develop a written business plan. He is too busy closing sales to worry about planning for the future.
- *Mistake #7.* Jerry has not formalized his management practices because he personally handles most of the client service and planning. He enjoys being Mr. Wonderful.
- *Mistake #8.* Jerry is counting on selling his practice to help fund his retirement, yet he has failed to develop an exit strategy based on the real value of his practice.

Until now, I've outlined strategies that will enhance the value of your business and make it more appealing to a buyer. But here's an added bonus: *You don't have to sell your practice at all.* If you institutionalize your business, you can walk away and continue to take an income stream—and live a much more fulfilling life. And isn't that what creating your own business is all about?

STOP Icons: When you see a stop sign, I want you to take time out from reading to look inward, taking an inventory of yourself or your business. This time for reflection will enable you to compare or identify the same kind of problems in your own situation and recognize the possible need to change your situation. You may not identify with all of the problems outlined in this book. You'll have to reflect inwardly and decide whether or not a specific problem applies to you, and if it does, really pay attention to potential solutions.

Does your sales practice look like Jerry's?	Yes ☐	No ☐
Did you think your practice was worth a lot more than it might actually be worth?	Yes ☐	No ☐
Do you really have a high paying job and a business with little equity value?	Yes ☐	No ☐

3

The Planner with Professional Success, but Personal Frustration

Unfortunately, most readers will look at this book and think "great ideas," then put it down and forget about it. Few will do the work required to change. Change is hard. To be blunt, it's a grueling process that will probably involve everybody in your organization. You have to go back to the very beginning and focus on key questions, such as: What matters most to you in life? What is your personal definition of success? What do you hope to accomplish in your career? What do you hope to achieve through your practice?

Most business owners have approached this issue from the perspective of looking first at their business objectives, not their personal aspirations. They ask the questions out of order, and as a result, their planning is usually poor, which is why personal gratification continues to elude them. In reality, people own businesses in order to shape their personal destinies. So whatever your personal objectives are, make sure your business will enable you to accomplish them.

We often see a conflict between an owner's personal vision and his corporate objective. I recently developed a strategic plan for an advisor who started a planning business. Anne (not her real name) had become very successful very quickly, but she was also very unhappy. Her husband, Bob, a computer consultant, couldn't understand why she continually expressed how dissatisfied she was. Though only in her mid-thirties, Anne already had $800,000 in annual sales and $230,000 in profit after expenses, plus she was taking $250,000 in salary.

Of course, many advisors would be thrilled to bring in almost a half a million dollars from their practice, but Anne finds herself in a situation where her life is completely out of balance. Her business is robbing her personal life of everything worthwhile. She left a large financial firm and started her own practice in her home to spend time with her young children. Her objective was to work part-time two or three days a week. Instead, due to her success, she finds herself working ridiculous hours six or seven days a week with no time for her kids, her husband, or herself. Everything personal in Anne's life is left until the demands of the business are met, and like many business owners, she finds that the demands of the business are seldom, if ever, met.

She has five dedicated staff people to support her in her practice, but like many financial planners, she is not only the sole executive in her firm, she is personally responsible for accomplishing all of the high level, client-centered functions in her practice. She is truly the cog in the wheel, responsible for all of the business management, financial planning, and problem-solving functions as well as sales, marketing, relationship management, compliance oversight, etc. The list goes on and on.

Anne has reached the end of her rope and is ready to walk away from the business rather than continue to operate this way. Indeed, at one meeting, Anne took her office keys out of her pocket and threw them on the conference table. "I'm done," she announced. "You can keep this business."

The problem was easy for an outsider to identify. Anne's practice had grown beyond her management skills. She is a great advisor, but she isn't a great manager of a growing business. Like many business owners, Anne had not done any strategic planning and didn't know where to start. She'd had no training in business management.

When I asked her to describe her work week for me, she began, "Well, I probably work 12 hours a day . . ."

While that's not too bad for a growing practice, when I asked about weekends, Anne painted a grim picture. "On Saturday I work from 8 AM until 2 PM, and then after the kids go to bed, I do a little more. On Sunday, I work pretty much off and on all day."

"What you're telling me is you're working seven days a week. So, when you go on vacation . . ."

She began to laugh, and I knew why. Vacation? Anne couldn't even take a day off; she was constantly in touch with her office.

We see that Anne, like Jerry, is making some of the common mistakes:

- *Mistake #1.* Anne channels all of her clients' service and advice through her. As a result, Anne's life is not only unmanageable, her clients see little value in the rest of her organization.
- *Mistake #2.* Anne has focused on gross revenue, not recurring revenue. While Anne has a large practice, fee-based assets under management are generating only 25 percent of her revenue, and she continues to generate a significant portion of her revenues through commissions.
- *Mistake #4.* Anne's personal vision doesn't match her corporate objective. While she has been very successful in growing her business, Anne finds little or no fulfillment in her personal life.
- *Mistake #7.* More and more clients want an advisor to provide them with comprehensive financial planning on a fee basis. Yet, Anne has been focused on investment planning and is still primarily operating under the old commission-based model.
- *Mistake #8.* Anne didn't have a written business plan to guide her business operations.
- *Mistake #10.* Anne didn't institutionalize her business through carefully developed management practices. Instead, she personally handles all of the high priority functions required in her business.
- *Mistake #12.* Anne was ready simply to close the doors to her business.

This is what happens when a business gets out of control. When we first begin our practice, we rarely envision working 60, 70, or 80 hours a week to achieve our goal. Quite the opposite, in fact—we expect to have more time away from the office to do the things we most enjoy. Of course, we also want to make a lot of money.

Many entrepreneurs start with a vision of what they need to do for their business to succeed, and this creates immediate tension. They work for their business; their business doesn't work for them. Like Anne, they find their professional lives appear successful, but their personal lives feel like a failure.

What if I told you it's possible to work less, but earn more? It's true—with proper planning. I know a few advisors who work only a couple of days a week and make $200,000 or $300,000 a year. They can do that because they've adopted *Personal Vision Planning,* a method that helps identify personal goals and develop a strategy for achieving them.

Have you ever promised yourself that tomorrow you will get around to living your life? Tomorrow, you say, you'll spend more time with your family and friends and do the things that will make you personally happy. Of course, tomorrow never comes. There's always one more project or plan that must be completed, one more sale that must be closed. All too often, everything personal is left until the demands of business are satisfied. Trouble is, the demands of a business are seldom, if ever, satisfied.

To avoid that trap, start with a vision of what you want your personal life to look like, then figure out how your business can help you make that dream a reality. Your practice is not the priority; it is only a facilitator to help you achieve your personal goals. *Your life is the priority.* That one thought seems to help me maintain perspective. Personal Vision Planning is the process of balancing personal priorities and business goals.

What are *your* personal priorities? You're not sure of the answer? Well, now's the time to find out!

Personal Vision Planning

4

Creating the Life You've Always Wanted

Even if you've been in business for years, Personal Vision Planning will help you determine who you really want to be, where you really want to go, and what you really want to accomplish in your life. Once you've figured that out, you can incorporate your findings in your business plan so that your professional life will enhance, not undermine, your personal life.

Here's a step that will help move you toward discovering the answer. First, find a quiet place where you won't be disturbed. This exercise requires intense and sustained concentration; it's not something you can do at the office between phone calls or after dinner while watching television. I'm lucky because I have a wonderful retreat in Canada where I can hide out. It's in the woods, right on the edge of a lake, and it's very quiet—the perfect spot for self-renewal. I usually spend a few days there each year evaluating what I'd like to get out of life. I find removing myself from day-to-day workplace pressures absolutely critical to gaining some perspective on what is really important to me. I answer the same questions every year: How much time do I want to spend with my family? Exactly how important are they to me, and what am I willing to give up to spend more time with them? I think that I'm supposed to be nurturing my family and making sure they know they're the most important part of my life, but like most business owners, I sometimes put business interests first.

It's very easy to convince ourselves that by putting business first and creating greater financial success, we really are taking care of our families. We're showing them how important they are by providing them with everything they need and want.

Don't you believe it. Every time we make something a higher priority than our loved ones, they notice. I was the son of a business owner, so I know what it's like. I personally decided that I was

Personal Vision Planning

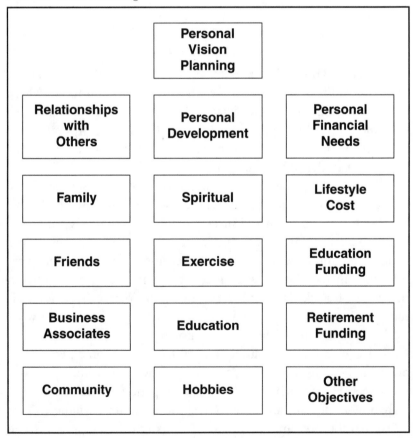

going to place my family first. My Personal Vision Planning is the anchor that keeps my life from drifting—and yours can be, too.

One of the greatest benefits of owning your own business is the opportunity to shape your own destiny. It is this very idea of self-determination that drives people to step out on their own. Without a clear idea of where you're going, though, how will you know when you've arrived? Indeed, how will you even know if you're on the right track?

You must articulate your life's goals so that you can create a path to help you reach them. The following questions will help you, but don't be discouraged if the answers don't come right away. You may have to go through the questionnaire several times before you're able to bring some definition and clarity to your vision—especially if you've only had a vague idea of your aspirations until now. But once you complete the questionnaire, you've taken the first step toward creating the kind of life you've always wanted.

One final reminder: As you answer the questions that follow, focus on where you want to be in the *future*—not where you are now.

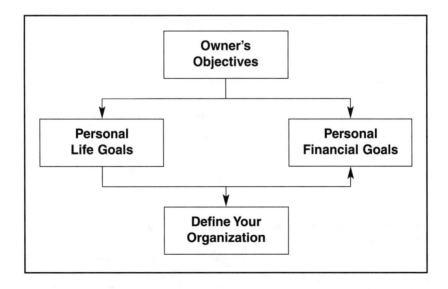

 PERSONAL VISION PLANNING
QUESTIONNAIRE

Part 1) Personal Life Goals (away from Work):

What do you want your life to look like?

_____

_____

Where do you want to live?

_____

_____

What does your ideal home look like?

_____

_____

What kind of car(s) do you want to drive?

_____

_____

Where do you want your children to go to school (or where do
they want to go to school)?

_____

_____

Who do you wish to be when you finally grow up?

_____

_____

How do you want to be remembered by your family? By your friends? By your business associates?

_____

_____

_____

How important is your family to you? How much time do you want to spend with them? What special things do you want to do for them, with them? How about your friends?

_____

_____

_____

How do you wish to spend your personal time? Do you have any hobbies or special interests that you'd like to pursue? Do you wish to devote more time to your spiritual needs? Exercise? Personal development?

_____

_____

How much vacation time do you take in a year? Where do you go and with whom?

_____

_____

What does your lifestyle look like? How often do you dine out? Hobbies, etc.?

_____

_____

What would you like to be doing three years from now? Five years
from now? Ten years from now?

_____

_____

_____

Part 2) Personal Financial Goals:

These next few questions may be best answered through the development of a personal financial plan with the help of a financial advisor.

How much money will you need to do the things you wish to do?
How much do you need now? In three years? In five years? In ten
years?

_____

_____

_____

What will it cost to educate your children? When is the money
needed, and how will you pay for their education?

_____

_____

When do you want to be financially independent? Where will the
money come from?

_____

_____

When do you want to retire? How much do you need to spend per
month to live the way you want? How much do you have invested?

How much do you need to save? What rate of return is required to accomplish your objective?

_____

_____

_____

How financially dependent are you on the continued and/or future success of your business?

_____

_____

_____

Part 3) Personal Life Goals (at Work):

What does your ideal work week look like?

_____

_____

How many hours do you work?

_____

What are your responsibilities?

_____

_____

What do you enjoy doing most?

_____

_____

What are you good at?

_____

_____

What do you like doing least?

_____

_____

When do you want to exit the business? How?

_____

_____

What will the value of your interest in the business be worth? Will this be enough to create financial independence? If not, what is your overall plan?

_____

_____

For an example, let's take a look at Anne's process of developing her Personal Vision Statement and strategic business plan.

Anne ranked her personal priorities as follows:

1. Spend quality time daily with her children.
2. Spend more quality time with her husband.
3. Make a significant contribution of her time to her church and the community.
4. Exercise daily.
5. Enrich her life by actually taking at least three vacations per year and traveling abroad.
6. Continue to live in their home.
7. Spend as many weekends at their shore home as possible.

8. Continue to send her children to private schools.
9. Be financially independent within ten years.

Anne's Personal Financial Goals:

1. Continue to maintain current lifestyle, spending $15,000 per month after taxes.
2. Be able to retire within ten years, with targeted spendable retirement income of $12,000 per month adjusted for inflation.
3. Provide $30,000 per year (adjusted for inflation) per child in college education funding.
4. Be able to sell the business within three to five years. (Anne is depending on the sale of the business to help fund her retirement.)

Anne's Personal Life Goals at Work:

1. After some extensive soul searching, she indicated she would be willing to work no more than five days a week, eight hours a day for the next six months. After that, she would be willing to work four days a week for the balance of the year, and then she would be willing to work only three days a week.
2. She wants to concentrate on what she enjoys doing most, working with clients to solve their financial problems.
3. She does not want to get involved in the day-to-day management of her practice. She has decided to hire someone to run her practice, and she's decided to add additional management support to ease her other responsibilities.
4. She wants to be in a position to sell the business or walk away in three to five years.
5. By adding additional management infrastructure to her practice, she believes she will be able to sell her business for about two times revenue.

When Anne viewed her completed Personal Vision Statement, she was shocked to see the divergence between what she wants her life to look like and the reality of her day-to-day existence. I assured her that she was not alone in her predicament—many business owners who have not gone through the rigors of creating a business plan find their personal and business lives in conflict. Now that she is armed with her personal vision statement, she has, for the first time, a tool to reengineer her business so that it acts as a facilitator in accomplishing her personal goals.

These may sound like insurmountable and costly changes for Anne to make, but when you look at how much time Anne was working, and the fact that she was ready to walk away from a net annual profit of nearly $500,000, we see that she has demonstrated she has ample resources and energy to put toward realizing her vision.

Having created her road map for success with her vision statement, Anne is well on her way to being able to exit her business within five years, selling it for at least two times revenue, helping to ensure her and her husband's future financial security and to guarantee a comfortable retirement. A personal vision statement that outlines what you want your life to look like, as well as a personal financial plan to determine the financial requirements such a life will cost, should guide you through the next step—defining your organization as an expression and facilitator of your personal vision.

5

Defining Your Organization

The reason I decided to become a financial planner almost 20 years ago, and not become a stockbroker or insurance agent, was because of the significant value that comprehensive, client-specific financial planning delivers. I have translated my personal philosophy into our mission statement and corporate philosophy.

Our corporate mission statement is *to develop advisory relationships, providing value-added advice and management to clients, which will enable them to achieve their goals.* Each and every person at my firm knows that the best interests of the clients come first—always. We have a relationship with our clients based on trust, and we will not do anything that might betray this trust. It's simply not worth it.

Your *mission statement* defines the purpose of your organization. It may be helpful to define exactly what we mean by using a standard dictionary definition: *The business with which a body of persons is charged.*

Some useful tips:

- Your mission statement should reflect your personal vision and your unique purpose for starting your business in the first place.

Defining the Organization

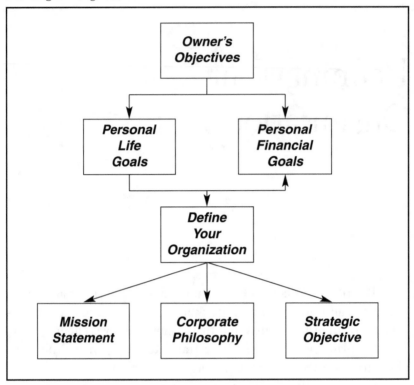

- Your mission statement should be clear and concise.
- Your mission statement should communicate your purpose to anyone who reads it.
- Your mission statement should not refer to specifics such as plans, products, or markets.

 Here are some basic points to consider:

What is the purpose of your organization?

_____

_____

What is your goal for your business?

_____

_____

_____

How will you know when you have reached your goal?

_____

_____

_____

     The mission statement defines your ultimate goal, but the _corporate philosophy_ defines your values—what your business truly stands for, and the way you go about achieving that goal. Also crucial to the success of your organization is a corporate philosophy that is explained to—and embraced by—everyone associated with your firm. It is an essential part of institutionalizing your business. It also helps ensure that your clients enjoy a consistent, high-quality experience every time they do business with your firm, regardless of who handles their account or answers their questions.

    A firm's mission statement may be to achieve the highest possible returns for its investors, but if the corporate philosophy is "by any means necessary" (legitimate or not-so-legitimate), that's a far different company than one whose mission is to achieve the highest returns possible but whose philosophy is to maintain ethical standards that are beyond reproach.

    For example, our corporate philosophy, or core belief, is that we must add value to each client's situation greater than their cost to retain us. This thread is woven throughout our business model and ties everything together. This focus on adding value has helped us stay the course and maintain our discipline of providing clients with financial planning services, while many other successful financial planners over the past five years have changed their focus to provide only investment management and advice.

Your philosophy should be simple, straightforward, and as easy as *A-B-C:*

- *Actions.* Actions speak louder than words. Your actions in relation to your stated values and standards will let others know if you are truly committed to them.
- *Beliefs.* Do not say anything you do not believe and do not intend to enforce.
- *Communication.* Clearly communicate your corporate philosophy to everyone in your organization and everyone with whom you do business.

You'd be amazed at how many firms don't bother to communicate the corporate philosophy below the level of vice president, or who publish it in an employee handbook that few people ever bother to read. Yet, who's the first employee that most clients and prospects see? It's the receptionist, and his or her actions must reflect the corporate philosophy. Otherwise, clients may come away thinking your philosophy is merely a marketing tool, something that sounds nice but really isn't embraced by your employees. You do not want to send that message. Ever.

Put your corporate philosophy in writing and discuss it with each employee when they're hired and during their annual (or semiannual) review. In fact, the degree to which the employee embodies the corporate philosophy should be a factor in their career advancement.

Your corporate philosophy can develop and strengthen over time. It does not have to be wordy or long. It may only state two or three things you feel strongly about and want everyone to know about your organization. Here is an excerpt from our corporate philosophy at Wealth Builders, Inc.:

- We are fiduciaries. Our clients' interests come first.
- We take what we do for our clients seriously, because they cannot afford to have us make mistakes.

- We add value to each client's situation significantly greater than the cost to retain us.
- We believe that greater knowledge is the key to developing innovative products and services.

A word of caution: Don't write down anything you don't personally believe and plan to live by yourself. Your employees will measure your actions to determine if you really believe what you have written. Your personal actions will determine if your organization will actually adopt and be defined by your philosophy statements.

The final step in defining your organization is to develop your *strategic objective*. Your strategic objective defines how you are going to direct your organization's resources to achieve your ultimate goal.

This objective is long range—five or more years out in the future. But to accomplish this ultimate objective, you will need to break your strategy down into strategic goals that can be easily communicated and measured. These are short range—one to three years in duration.

Our strategic goals are:

- To be a leader in providing value added financial advisory and business planning services to individuals and institutions.
- To leverage the use of technology to provide an extremely high level of profit to the company, while providing a level of quality and service to our clients that our competitors cannot duplicate.
- To concentrate the company's resources in perfecting and expanding our three core business units.

Analyzing your personality style and your personal vision is extremely important when developing a strategic business objective for your company. The type of business you are in should not determine your values; rather, your values should define and govern your business. The process we've been outlining might reveal that the type of business you are building is diametrically opposed to your values and goals and will actually prevent you from realizing your personal vision. How can this happen?

6

Matching Your Objectives to the Business

At first glance, all owners would seem to have pretty much the same objective: to create a successful company that makes them rich. In talking to hundreds of business owners over the past 20 years we have found that they tell us pretty much the same thing over and over again:

- They want to own their own business so that they can control their own destiny. They feel in many cases that they have not had the opportunity to make decisions, influencing others on the way to making a difference in the their corner of the world.
- They also tell us that they would like more personal freedom, to have the flexibility to work when they want to, schedule their own hours, not to be at someone else's beck and call.
- Yes, and they want to attain financial independence by building a business that has significant equity value. They want their piece of the American dream, and they view owning a business as the best way to get there.

In probing further, however, many business owners find it difficult to clearly identify their objectives because of the mix of conflicting personal and business goals. The goals you set will depend not only on your personal life goals, but also on what type of business owner you are, and what type of business you want to run.

You Own Your Own Business!

"The American Dream"

When we ask our business owner clients why they choose to *own* a business . . . They tell us . . .

- "To control my own destiny"
- "To create personal freedom"
- "To attain financial independence by building a business that has *significant equity value*"

So . . . How's it going so far?

For example, some individuals want to start a business in the hope that a few years down the line it will be doing well enough financially so that they can take time off to play golf or go on long vacations. Others want the challenge of managing a fast growing business, with the challenges of constantly changing people, rapid changes in technology, product development, and marketing problems. Still others want something in between. Taking business and personal needs together, you will likely discover that your personality matches one or several of the following categories.

Startup specialist. This is the person who thrives on the business creation process. The startup specialist develops products and gets his or her team through the first few years, then after building a stabilized business turns the company over to professional managers. In the business startup game, of course, those first years not only determine survival but the ultimate long-term success of the business.

The startup specialist loves to put the pieces of the business together: making a prototype product, assembling a management team, obtaining financing, and wooing potential customers. Once the business is together and working the way it was intended, startup specialists begin to lose interest. What they most want to move on to, not surprisingly, is another new venture. The most common way of doing that is to sell their interest in the company and use the proceeds to start the next business.

Professional business manager. This individual wants to start or buy a business and stay with it through his or her life and the company's life. That means building and managing the business through all the company's stages, from startup and survival to profitability. If the entrepreneur is fortunate, it may also mean building a world-class business that has a strong enough management team and infrastructure to take the company public or transfer it to the next generation.

The best-of-both-worlds entrepreneur. This person is kind of a cross between the startup specialist and the professional business manager. Like the startup specialist, the best-of-both-worlds entrepreneur starts a company with the idea of selling it down the road for a capital gain. Like the professional business manager, once this individual gets the cash from the buyout, he or she ideally would like to stay on to continue to guide the company using these expanded resources. The best-of-both-worlds entrepreneur, thus, wants both the financial rewards of selling a successful company and the professional/ego rewards of continuing to guide the company through future stages of growth.

The hard part of the equation for many entrepreneurs is that running the business for someone else just is not as much fun as running it for themselves. Also, sharing authority with an outsider is not something many entrepreneurs do very well (often, this is the very reason they left corporate life to strike out on their own). Studies have shown that less than half of acquired management stay with their companies more than three years. Only in those cases in which the acquiring company truly leaves the original management team alone can the arrangement work well.

The business engineer. This person views the fledgling business as a kind of laboratory for concocting new products, perfecting business processes, or entire business models. Professionals who've become frustrated with their work in large corporations or as consultants often decide that the best way to achieve control of their own destiny is simply to start their own companies. Such entrepreneurs seem to have unusually clear vision and a unique ability to identify and solve problems, to create a far more efficient business process. However, they often find that they are not good business managers. They often have the best chance of succeeding when they recognize their managerial weaknesses and have the good sense to bring in professional managers to run the business.

Lifestyle business owner. This individual mainly wants the business to provide as nice a living as possible. Essentially, the business becomes a funding vehicle that enables the entrepreneur to take exotic vacations and buy multiple vacation homes, expensive cars, a yacht—in general, to enjoy all the good life has to offer. If possible to attain the lifestyle of the rich and famous. Lifestyle business owners do not want the business to get too big, because fast growth means problems. These owners do not want to have to worry about obtaining additional financing or hiring or managing too many employees, to achieve the lifestyle they desire they want to keep their business life as simple as possible.

Do you see yourself and your management style in one or more of these profiles? If so, then use that information to fine-tune your company's objectives. For example, if you realize that, deep down, you're really a lifestyle business owner, then it makes no sense to set aggressive growth goals, because that will mean devoting more of your time to the business—something you probably don't want to do. Similarly, if you discover that you are a startup specialist, then your goals should be directed toward making your business an appealing acquisition target.

Once you've identified your personality profile, you can accurately identify the appropriate strategic business objective. Possibilities include:

- *Going public.* Some entrepreneurs set their company's sights on going public. This is considered the ultimate goal for a business builder, the American dream, a major milestone of success. Few ever attain this goal, but those who achieve this objective are considered modern day heroes and are often heralded in the press. Going public can also accomplish several desirable business goals simultaneously. It can provide a method for outside investors to cash out and achieve the capital gain they sought when they invested. It also enables the company to raise funds to fuel further growth and expand product or service offerings. Going public is a reasonable juncture signaling the departure of a startup specialist or a milestone in the life of the professional business managers. Personalities most compatible with this goal are startup specialists, professional business managers, and some business engineers (those with the good sense to bring in experienced executives).

- *Becoming a large corporation.* This is probably the most common fantasy of entrepreneurs. They expect their company will experience phenomenal growth and become a major corporation, like an IBM, Dell, or Microsoft.

  In order to become a large corporation, the entrepreneur's business plan must prove that this objective is realistic. Documenting the owner's previous business experience usually does this most convincingly. Those who have previously started successful companies or managed effectively in large companies are the most likely candidates for future success and make the most convincing cases based on their past experience. Corporate managers who have helped guide a new product or service successfully to market or started a new division are more likely to impress financial backers. Personalities most compatible with this goal are professional business managers.

- *Being acquired.* Many companies are started with the explicit goal of being acquired five to ten years or longer down the road, after they have become accepted in the marketplace, and become profitable. Many financial planning and investment management firms are considering this as a potential exit strategy. The acquirer can be a major financial corporation; a smaller, diversified planning group; or a group of investors looking to take over a promising growth business. Venture capitalists will understand and approve this goal, because it offers them an opportunity to cash out, while potentially achieving the capital appreciation they desire. Personalities most compatible with this goal are startup specialists who are ready to move on, or the best-of-both-worlds entrepreneur who will use the cash-out to fund retirement and lifestyle needs.

- *Becoming a niche company.* Some companies adeptly carve out a narrow slice of a market—some specialty product or service—that would not interest many other competitors. They increase revenue and profits by 10 to 20 percent annually, achieving anywhere between $5 million and $10 million in sales. The owners are satisfied with the challenge of perfecting the products and services they offer to clients in their niche and look to gain a dominant position in their market. Personalities most compatible with this goal are professional business managers or business engineers.

- *Becoming a partner in a joint venture.* For entrepreneurs, especially those involved in relatively small financial services businesses, a joint venture with a major corporation who can provide them with needed financial and marketing muscle can be a powerful and attractive enticement. Becoming involved with a large company as a partner in a joint venture will give a new business instant credibility and vast resources.

However, negotiating joint venture agreements can be a tedious and lengthy process, and to be successful both parties must focus on common objectives. Joint ventures can also be structured between smaller companies that can gain competitive advantage through a collaborative combination. Personalities most compatible with this goal are professional business managers, business engineers (those who are adept at working closely with corporate types or who can find a negotiator to perform this service), and even startup specialists—but only if there is some provision for this individual to sell out a few years down the road.

- *Being a cash cow.* No rule says business owners must build companies that continually grow in sales and profits. Companies can be started with the objective of achieving a certain size and then milking the profits. The profits might be used to support the owner's current lifestyle or retirement expenses, or to start new businesses as well as to acquire other ventures. Personalities most compatible with this goal are lifestyle business owners who would continue to use the business to fund their desired lifestyles.
- *Acquiring other companies.* Some owners develop acquisition plans with the goal of building up miniconglomerates. They may specialize in acquiring financially troubled smaller companies and turning them around, or they may prefer similar companies across a particular geographic area. Personalities most compatible with this goal are startup specialists and professional business managers.

You will save yourself a lot of time and energy if you determine your personality profile and compatible professional goals before drawing up your strategic business plan. You will also have a much greater chance to stay the course for success if you are realistic about what you can accomplish and the environment you need to succeed.

We have found that business owners who fail to integrate their personal vision and their business objectives often end up with a nightmare instead of the what they perceived as the American dream of controlling their own destiny, achieving financial freedom, and achieving financial independence through equity creation. They often find themselves in the same position in which Anne finds herself, with a business that is robbing her of her life, a business that is wholly dependent on her for success, a high paying job, and a business with little or no equity value.

The Dream and the Reality

If This Is the American Dream . . . "Will somebody please wake me up!"

The Dream	The Reality
You control your destiny	x You're great at crisis management
You have personal freedom	x Your business is your life
Your business has significant equity value	x You have a sales practice, which has little equity value
You have achieved financial independence	x You are completely, financially dependent on your business

By carefully integrating your personal vision of what you want your personal life to look like, with your personality type and business objective, you can actually experience the American dream, a business that facilitates a rewarding personal life, while providing you with the financial success that you have only dreamed of.

7

Your Road Map to Success

So you've identified your personal vision, and you've established your mission statement, corporate philosophy, and strategic objective—at least in your mind. But if you haven't written down your conclusions, then your work is not done.

Remember Mistake #6? Many business models fail because the owner doesn't stick with a business plan. One of the main reasons for failure is that the owner fails to put the plan in writing. But by drawing up a written business plan, you create a synthesis of your personal goals in your business. When you document the process, others in your company can follow it.

Over the years, I have witnessed the destruction of business after business because the owners did not have a written business plan to guide operations, allocate resources effectively, and keep company executives and corporate resources committed to achieving the organization's strategic objective. Without a written plan, owners are often seduced into abandoning their current business model for the latest get-rich-quick fad.

Some years ago, we were building an independent financial planning broker-dealer. One of the most successful financial planning groups we recruited was owned by two extremely seasoned

Your Road Map to Success

Your Personal Vision Defines:
> Corporate Mission
> Corporate Philosophy
> Strategic Objective

Strategic Business Plan

professionals, Jeff and Rob. They had a total of nine salespeople (including themselves) and five support staff. Their group was generating in excess of $2,000,000 of gross dealer concessions by giving quarterly financial planning seminars to the public. They teamed up with a New York financial radio personality, and their seminars were so highly regarded, they began to limit the number of seminar attendees to 250.

Jeff and Rob had developed a unique marketing model that was providing them with more interested, qualified prospects than they could handle. They offered each seminar participant a free one-hour, no obligation financial planning consultation in their office, and they were converting about 40 new clients per month while holding one seminar per quarter.

Jeff and Rob were pretty satisfied with the way their business was running. Their only complaint was that the average client from the seminar had only $100,000 to invest—not enough, they thought, to justify the expense of the seminar and all the work that went into the financial plan. They started looking for a new method of obtaining clients that would ensure they penetrated a more affluent market segment.

Over a period of months, Jeff and Rob decided to give up the seminar business and try to penetrate the professional market. They met with a multilevel marketing group concentrating on selling doctors and dentists "private pension plans," using single premium life insurance as the funding vehicle. Professionals could set up these plans for themselves without including their employees, keeping all the contributions for themselves. The potential insurance commissions were enormous, according to their marketing group.

Lured by a more affluent client base and visions of greater income, Jeff and Rob completely abandoned the seminar/financial planning business model. Over the next few years, we watched as their business fell apart, their gross commissions plummeted from just over $2 million to $300,000. Because of the lack of revenue, all of the sales and most of the staff people were forced to find new jobs.

Jeff and Rob now found themselves trying to eke out a living where they once had one of the more successful financial planning practices in the country.

All businesses need to adapt and change in a competitive business environment, adjusting their plan accordingly, but we have found that radical change often destroys the business. Each of us needs to determine what we do well and stick with it until we perfect it.

To reiterate—you can avoid making *Mistake #6* by:

- Defining your strategic objective.
- Determining the short-range and mid-range goals required to accomplish your objective.
- Adopting a *written* strategy to ensure these goals are met.

STOP Even at this early stage of business plan development, most business owners feel rejuvenated, energized, and more excited about their personal and business lives than ever before. For most business owners, for probably the first time they have a clear vision of what they want most out of life, and now they want to apply this newfound information to make sure their business conforms to this vision.

At this point, the business owner has to resist trying to take a shortcut and implement solutions without having completely developed the business plan. They can see some of the problems and are eager to implement solutions. Because at this stage, they have only completed part of their plan, they have only part of the picture, and any problems they try to solve are likely to lead to new mistakes.

This happened to Anne (see Chapter 3) as she recognized some of her basic problems and rushed to find solutions.

Determined to solve *Mistake #1,* Anne recognized she needed to hire some additional executive and sales talent to institutionalize her practice. A Vice President of Operations would require compensation of approximately $100,000 per year. Anne would also hire and train a salesperson/planner to interface with existing clients, providing advice and service, to begin shifting the focal point of the business away from her and onto the business. We recommended that new salespeople be hired as salaried employees, so the projected cost for a new sales associate was approximately $50,000 plus additional bonuses based on performance.

AT THIS POINT, WE ADVISED ANNE TO STOP!

Anne had identified the need to hire the additional managerial and sales talent and determined that she was willing to reinvest some of her current income to fund these expenses and generate sales. However, she hadn't realized that she was committing herself to continue to work the same hours she had been working. Without a completed written business plan, she was going to be right back where she started, only now she had to generate the same level of sales while training two new employees. Out of the frying pan into the fire!

If you're going to build a business that doesn't require your being there, then your employees must be empowered to make top-level decisions. A written business plan communicates how you want things in your organization to get done. Otherwise, getting your staff to share your commitment is really hard when they don't know your goals. Once you list and explain those goals and your staff's role in the process, then you don't have to know what each employee is doing every day. They know what they have to do, and they are empowered to do it.

Our objective in this section has been to help you define your organization and create a road map for success. If you have diligently developed your personal vision (what you really want out of life) and translated it into a new definition of what your business needs to do, you are well on your way to institutionalizing your sales practice into a world-class business with significant value.

As with all planning, you'll derive the greatest benefits when you analyze the big picture and integrate global solutions. The next step is to analyze your practice or business in depth and determine what you need to do to allow the business to give you what you want out of life. *Part Three* is designed to help you clarify the scope of your endeavors by taking into account where you have come from, where you are headed, and the competitive forces affecting your business.

Creating a written business plan should yield many benefits over and above the actual document. Most importantly, you establish a planning process that you can use over and over again, improving it each time by incorporating the experience you have gained. Both the document and the process enable you to derive the maximum benefit from the work you put into creating the plan. A dynamic document should be kept current as your business evolves. Realistically, though, you're probably planning all the time.

Engineering a Business Plan

8

Corporate History

A corporate history gives you and your employees perspective about how long it took for you to get where you are today. It allows you to appreciate your accomplishments along the way and to set goals and strategies more reasonably in the future.

You need to set the stage for your business plan with a narrative that explains how your company came into being and what major milestones you've passed. This story will give you a sense of why you chose the business you're in and where you currently stand in the business lifecycle, and it will provide a general overview of your major strengths and weaknesses. This section of the business plan need not be lengthy and filled with facts and figures. The emphasis should be on conveying the broad outline in a way that presents a very positive image of your company. It's a good opportunity for you to express your personal style.

This is your workbook section. Start by answering the following questions about your business. Take as much time as you need to recall the facts. The information you assemble may contain some pleasant surprises and will surely enlighten you to what may have been false starts, wrong or too many directions, or simply some unnecessary efforts.

What is the date and location where your business was started?

_____

What is your current location, if different?

_____

What is the form of organization? Sole proprietor, C Corporation, S Corporation, Partnership, LLC?

_____

Who are the founders and other key people involved?

_____

_____

What do they bring to the business?

_____

_____

Why did you start your business?

_____

_____

What problems have you encountered?

_____

_____

How were they overcome or resolved?

_____

_____

What were the key milestones achieved since you started your business?

_____

_____

How were these milestones accomplished?

_____

_____

How did you identify and penetrate your market?

_____

_____

How have you dealt with the competition?

_____

_____

What are the strengths and weaknesses of your business?

_____

_____

How much has been invested in the business? What was the source of funding?

_____

_____

How has the money been used?

_____

_____

Re-create your financials. What were your revenues, expenses, and profit for each year you have been in business?

_____

_____

Now summarize this information in a format that highlights the foundation you have built to support your future *superstructure*.

9

Industry Analysis

The CEO's job is to direct and focus resources to accomplish the company's strategic objective. A thorough analysis and an accurate knowledge of your industry is essential.

We have found the key to analyzing our industry is to stay aware of recent trends. We read everything we can get our hands on and glean information from daily news, weekly and monthly financial industry magazines, articles, research reports, and books.

Notice how some of these recent trends alert you to adjust your course:

- *Increased prevalence of mutual funds, including no-loads.* More than 12,000 mutual funds now exist in the United States; in comparison, only about 8,000 stocks actively trade.
- *No transaction fee supermarkets.* Mutual funds have become a commodity for most investors, and asset allocation is quickly following suit. Because allocation has been many planners' unique selling proposition to investors, their perceived value is vanishing.

- *Low or no transaction costs through the Internet.* Trading that can be done almost free over the Internet leaves little room for price advantage in our offerings.
- *Dramatic increase in access to information.* The Internet and personal finance media have given consumers access to information that in the past was available only to professionals at high cost. The days of being needed for access to knowledge are over.
- *Bull market performance.* Investors are lulled by favorable returns into thinking they can "do it themselves."

Consider our evolution. In the early 1980s, we wrote elaborate, comprehensive financial plans for clients. This process was painful because manufacturing the plan took so long (the software was not what it is today). Presenting the plan would take four or more hours, and factoring in client changes involved even more time and effort.

Then came the late 1980s. Many planners rushed to find tax shelters for their clients, and traditional financial planning was forsaken as planners emphasized tax savings through partnerships. Well, we all know that approach didn't work out very well for clients—or planners who had to reinvent themselves in the public's mind. They did this by going back to the basics in the early 1990s, but that approach didn't last long, either.

In the latter half of the '90s, advisors were urged to move away from traditional comprehensive planning practices. Thanks to breakthroughs in technology, financial planning had gone high tech. It had become modular: rather than fit the plan to the client, planners now attempted to fit the client to prepackaged investment or retirement planning modules. Of course, banks, brokerages, and other institutions didn't take long to realize that they could do this, too. Moreover, they had brand-name recognition and marketing muscle, with which sole practitioners couldn't hope to compete.

Impersonal corporations were taking the very profession that planners had developed away from them, or so it seemed to many advisors. What they failed to realize was that they themselves had come to be perceived as impersonal corporations. They'd lost the personal touch.

We need to work diligently in order to participate in the new direction of our industry. With the increase in competition and decrease in our perceived value, we truly have only three opportunities:

1. *Product superiority.* However, to compete against major Wall Street firms in this area would require research and development (R&D) budgets larger than most of our total assets under management.
2. *Price.* To make this work requires the scale of players such as Vanguard, Schwab, and Fidelity.
3. *Customer service.* Study after study has shown that individuals want an ongoing relationship with a trusted professional who can integrate their investment, business, financial, and estate matters consistent with their life goals.

The obvious choice for most advisors is to compete on value (customer service). Fortunately, we are in a natural position to increase our value dramatically by going back to the basics and offering financial planning services, which many of us forsake in favor of asset management.

Today, financial planning means spending enough time with the client's data, goals, and objectives to become an expert on the client's situation, thereby ensuring goal achievement for the client. If we reintroduce financial planning as a high-quality experience so that our clients perceive greater value from us than from our competitors, we will succeed. The challenge is to deliver this experience systematically to each one of our clients every time and still *maintain profitability.*

At a minimum, you need to examine answers to the following questions before deciding how best to position your company's strengths:

Identify your industry. How big is it? Revenues? Profits?

_____

_____

Who are the major industry participants?

_____

_____

Who is most competitive? Rank the top 20 players.

_____

_____

Estimate their market share.

_____

_____

What advantages do you have over them?

_____

_____

What part of the market do you fit into?

_____

_____

How will you capture clients that others are competing for?

_____

_____

How is the industry changing?

_____

_____

Where is it expected to be in five years? Ten years?

_____

_____

Will your market share increase or decrease with these changes? Why?

_____

_____

Who is the right client? That depends on you—your personal vision and business objectives. Let's see if we can identify the segment that's right for you.

ow will you satisfy their needs or wants better than the competition?

hat share of the market do you hope to capture? (Locally, re-
onally, nationally?)

ow will you increase and defend your market share?

ow will you attract new customers?

ow will the needs of this target market change over the next three
five years?

You'll want to identify your ideal client niche as narrowly as
ssible, keeping in mind that your niche must be large enough to
port your company profitably. The driving force behind niche
rketing is the need to satisfy and retain those consumers who re-
love your services. To continue selling to the same clients is
ch more efficient than to go out continually and find new ones.

The point is to focus your efforts, not only on how you plan
penetrate your market, but how you will ultimately defend it.

10

Target Market Analysis

Everybody talks about the baby boomers becoming the wealthiest generation ever, but I've found that seniors, the parents of the
boomers, are not that worried about their children. The boomers
are doing pretty well for themselves; in fact, many seniors are appalled at the way their kids spend money. Rather, seniors are more
worried about their grandkids. They often ask us to set up plans to
bypass their children, giving the money to their grandchildren to
ensure their financial futures.

I believe this is one of the greatest opportunities for financial
planners. If you're going to get the money and keep the money,
then you have to do some generational wealth planning. If you get
the money at the senior level, then you get to manage it through
the next several generations and ensure the continued success of
your practice.

Seniors control approximately two-thirds of the money invested
in the United States, and they are predominantly delegators. They
look for someone to provide them with turnkey financial advice and
management across all areas of their financial life. They're not particularly price sensitive, so they're a very profitable target market.

They want to build a trusting relationship with an individual and/ or company that will provide them with this turnkey platform.

Studies also show that there are three million small businesses that will pass from one generation to another over the next five years. Small business owners in the United States represent the most affluent target market. They have relatively complex financial situations and, therefore, require a lot of help. This market segment is also comprised primarily of delegators: people who want a trustworthy, knowledgeable financial advisor to provide them with turnkey financial advice and management—someone who they can trust to be their financial quarterback. They are not particularly price sensitive and are willing to pay for top-quality advice.

Does your organization provide the level of advice and service these clients want? If not, you may want to reengineer your business to deliver turnkey financial services to one of these market segments.

You need to determine if enough prospects in your chosen market are willing to purchase what you have to offer, at the price you need to charge to make a profit. The best way to find out is to conduct a methodical analysis of the market you plan to reach. You may very well sell to several types of clients, so you'll want to describe the most important characteristics of each group separately.

The following questions will help you more clearly define and assess your target market and whether you are aligned to reach your sales goals:

Who or what is your target market? (Individuals, corporations, etc.)

_____

_____

Which clients are best suited to the services you provide?

_____

_____

What is the size of your target market? _____

Can your market be segmented? (Seniors, boomers, Xe owners, professionals, executives, retirees, etc.)

_____

_____

What market segments offer the greatest growth poter

_____

_____

What is the ideal profile of your target customer?

   a) Age _____

   b) Profession _____

   c) Income _____

   d) Geographic location _____

   e) Net worth _____

   f) Other defining demographics _____

What do these customers want?

_____

_____

What are the currents trends in the market?

_____

_____

What will be the impact on the customers who use yo services?

_____

_____

10

Target Market Analysis

Everybody talks about the baby boomers becoming the wealthiest generation ever, but I've found that seniors, the parents of the boomers, are not that worried about their children. The boomers are doing pretty well for themselves; in fact, many seniors are appalled at the way their kids spend money. Rather, seniors are more worried about their grandkids. They often ask us to set up plans to bypass their children, giving the money to their grandchildren to ensure their financial futures.

I believe this is one of the greatest opportunities for financial planners. If you're going to get the money and keep the money, then you have to do some generational wealth planning. If you get the money at the senior level, then you get to manage it through the next several generations and ensure the continued success of your practice.

Seniors control approximately two-thirds of the money invested in the United States, and they are predominantly delegators. They look for someone to provide them with turnkey financial advice and management across all areas of their financial life. They're not particularly price sensitive, so they're a very profitable target market.

They want to build a trusting relationship with an individual and/ or company that will provide them with this turnkey platform.

Studies also show that there are three million small businesses that will pass from one generation to another over the next five years. Small business owners in the United States represent the most affluent target market. They have relatively complex financial situations and, therefore, require a lot of help. This market segment is also comprised primarily of delegators: people who want a trustworthy, knowledgeable financial advisor to provide them with turnkey financial advice and management—someone who they can trust to be their financial quarterback. They are not particularly price sensitive and are willing to pay for top-quality advice.

Does your organization provide the level of advice and service these clients want? If not, you may want to reengineer your business to deliver turnkey financial services to one of these market segments.

You need to determine if enough prospects in your chosen market are willing to purchase what you have to offer, at the price you need to charge to make a profit. The best way to find out is to conduct a methodical analysis of the market you plan to reach. You may very well sell to several types of clients, so you'll want to describe the most important characteristics of each group separately.

The following questions will help you more clearly define and assess your target market and whether you are aligned to reach your sales goals:

Who or what is your target market? (Individuals, corporations, etc.)

_____

_____

Which clients are best suited to the services you provide?

_____

_____

What is the size of your target market? _____

Can your market be segmented? (Seniors, boomers, Xers, business owners, professionals, executives, retirees, etc.)

_____

_____

What market segments offer the greatest growth potential?

_____

_____

What is the ideal profile of your target customer?

    a) Age _____

    b) Profession _____

    c) Income _____

    d) Geographic location _____

    e) Net worth _____

    f) Other defining demographics _____

What do these customers want?

_____

_____

What are the currents trends in the market?

_____

_____

What will be the impact on the customers who use your product or services?

_____

_____

How will you satisfy their needs or wants better than the competition?

_____

_____

What share of the market do you hope to capture? (Locally, regionally, nationally?)

_____

How will you increase and defend your market share?

_____

_____

How will you attract new customers?

_____

_____

How will the needs of this target market change over the next three to five years?

_____

_____

You'll want to identify your ideal client niche as narrowly as possible, keeping in mind that your niche must be large enough to support your company profitably. The driving force behind niche marketing is the need to satisfy and retain those consumers who really love your services. To continue selling to the same clients is much more efficient than to go out continually and find new ones.

The point is to focus your efforts, not only on how you plan to penetrate your market, but how you will ultimately defend it.

Do you know how much your average client is worth to you?

- Age 55
- $500,000 in assets to invest
- Over 30 years

$847,401

We Know!

Is their business steady, increasing, or decreasing?

_____

_____

List the strengths and weaknesses of each.

_____

_____

_____

_____

How does your business compare to your competitor's?

   a) In length of time in business? _____

   b) In sales volume (units and dollars)? _____

   c) In size and number of employees, suppliers, and support
      personnel?

      _____

      _____

   d) In number of customers? Share of market? Product niche?

      _____

      _____

What are the similarities/dissimilarities between your business and
your competitor's business?

_____

_____

_____

_____

On what basis will you compete with them? (Check)

    [ ] product superiority

    [ ] price

    [ ] advertising

    [ ] technology/innovation

    [ ] other

In what aspect(s) is your business better? That is, what is your distinctive competence? (Check)

    [ ] operations

    [ ] management

    [ ] product

    [ ] price

    [ ] service

    [ ] delivery

    [ ] other

What have you learned by observing your competition?

_____

_____

_____

What competition will you meet in each product/service line?

_____

_____

How does your product/service compare with the competition in the eyes of customers?

_____

_____

What do you know about others like you who are not yet in the market?

_____

_____

Does your company have any technological advantages over your competition? If so, how will you exploit these advantages?

_____

_____

Though you may have identified the largest players in your industry, not all of these businesses will be competing directly with you. Some may be located in geographically distant locations. Therefore, in your analysis, you'll focus on those businesses that directly compete with you for sales.

It may help to think of your competitors as a series of levels, ranging from your most direct competitors to those who are more remote.

First level. Financial advisors and planners who are direct competitors with your service in your geographic locality. In many cases, these competitors offer a product or service that is interchangeable with yours in the eyes of the consumer (although, of course, you hope to hold the advantage).

Second level. Competitors who offer similar products in a different business category or who are more geographically remote.

Brokers, CPAs, online trading—this year alone, the top six firms will spend $1.6 billion advertising their name on radio, on TV, and in print. None of these competitors provides exactly the same mix of products and services as you, but they may be picking off the most lucrative parts of your business.

Third level. Providers of other types of products, such as insurance or bank-related products.

The point of this analysis is to consider carefully, from the buyer's point of view, all the alternatives. Knowing those, you can attempt to make sure that your business provides advantages over your competitors, beginning with those who are the most directly similar to you. In fact, you can even borrow ideas from second- or third-level competitors in order to compete more effectively against your first-tier competitors. When completed, a detailed analysis will show you where you need to concentrate your energies to make and keep your organization more competitive.

Use the charts on the next few pages to determine how competitive you believe your business to be compared to your competitors. This process will allow you to identify your company's strengths and weaknesses and illuminate the problem areas where you need to focus your attention. You may identify several competitive weaknesses that you feel you cannot solve by yourself. Don't be discouraged—contact your resource partners and ask for their help. If we are to survive and prosper, we will need to get our larger resource partners involved in our strategic planning to help us compete against larger, well capitalized competitors.

COMPETITIVE ANALYSIS How Do Clients Perceive Your Advice and Service?

Category Rank 1-10 (1=Low, 10=High)	Your Firm	Other Local Financial Planners	CPA Firms	Brokers	Banks
Service Menu and Benefits	10	8	7	6	5
Service Cost	6	7	4	5	8
Implementation Cost	9	7	6	5	3
Value Added Savings	9	8	8	5	4
Quality of Advice and Service	9	8	8	5	6
Perceived Value of Advice and Service	10	8	7	5	6
Image	7	6	6	8	9
Name Recognition	5	3	5	10	9
Customer Relationships (Trust)	10	9	8	6	6
Office Location	7	6	7	9	10
Delivery Time	8	6	5	3	4
Convenience of Use	10	9	7	6	10
Credit Policies	5	6	6	9	9
Customer Service	10	8	7	7	7
Social Image	8	7	8	7	10
Other:					
Total Points	123	106	99	96	106

Study your competitors' ads, brochures, and promotional materials. Drive past their offices. Talk to their clients. Wholesalers and reps can also provide rich information about competitors' strengths and weaknesses. What are they doing well that you can copy, and what are they doing poorly that you can capitalize on? Analyze each competitor's ability and speed of innovation for new products and services.

COMPETITIVE ANALYSIS How Do You Rank Your Firm against Competitors?

Category Rank 1-10 (1=Low, 10=High)	Your Firm	Other Financial Planners	CPA Firms	Brokers	Banks
Financial Resources	5	3	6	10	9
Marketing Program	5	4	3	10	8
Technological Competence	9	6	4	8	5
Access to Distribution	4	3	2	10	9
Access to Other Professionals	5	3	5	10	9
Economies of Scale	3	1	4	10	9
Operational Efficiencies	8	5	4	8	5
Sales Process/ Competence	10	8	5	7	3
Consulting Menu Breadth	9	6	6	7	5
Strategic Partnerships	5	3	4	10	7
Company Personnel	8	6	7	7	5
Knowledge Level	10	8	8	5	3
Certification/ Regulatory	8	6	4	9	5
Patents/ Trademarks	5	1	1	7	5
Industry Contacts	5	4	4	10	8
Other: Total Points	99	67	67	128	95

I can tell you from personal experience that failure to carefully measure your plans against the competition can be disastrous.

In the mid-1980s, we decided to expand our product and service distribution capabilities by creating an independent financial planning broker-dealer. The plan was to recruit reps away from the larger, product-oriented independents by offering reps access to our fee-based money management platform and financial planning business model. We knew our offering was superior, and we had developed great back office capability. Our only significant concern was whether we could compete against larger, well capitalized firms. With a larger capital base, these firms were perceived by reps to be more stable, and they had the budget to dominate recruiting through direct selling and advertising.

While we considered these factors, we did not do an in-depth analysis to determine if we could overcome these competitive disadvantages. We rationalized our concerns and decided to proceed with the formation of our broker-dealer.

We were doing quite well overcoming reps' objections that we were too small until Integrated Resources Equity Corporation (IREC) filed for bankruptcy protection. We thought this company's failure would be a recruiting windfall. We had been trying to recruit IREC reps for several years; surely now they would move to our firm. As it turned out, reps' concern over size and stability increased dramatically after IREC's failure. They told us they thought we had a great firm, but if IREC could fail, they surely did not want to move to a firm as small as ours. We sold our broker-dealer to a larger firm several years later, after failing to achieve critical mass.

I am sure if we had done a thorough analysis of the competition and business environment, we would have allocated our limited resources to increase profits in our other core businesses.

12

Products and Services Alignment

Once you've determined who your target market is and identified exactly what that market truly wants, you need to carefully analyze whether your products and services are actually delivering—delivering in such a way as to set you apart from your competition.

WHAT CONSUMERS PREFER: MOST RELIABLE SOURCE OF FINANCIAL INFORMATION

The following questions will help you determine if your offerings are the best they can be, and whether they are aligned with your clients' needs:

What is the purpose or benefit of each product or service offered, and how does it achieve this benefit?

_____

_____

What new products or services can you develop to meet the changing needs of the market?

_____

_____

What are its unique features or benefits?

_____

_____

What are the regulatory or approval requirements?

_____

_____

How will you manufacture and promote your products and services?

_____

_____

Can you protect your products or services through patents or trademarks?

_____

_____

How do you price your products and services? Are they competitive?

_____

_____

Have you identified the cost and profit margin of each product or service offering?

_____

_____

Have you broken down your revenue and profit goals by product and service?

_____

_____

Identifying exactly who we are going to do business with and what services we are going to provide enables us to develop a uniform service platform that streamlines our business. By building uniformity into service delivery, we can use technology to handle more clients and to deliver consistent services more efficiently at every level of our organization.

For example, we built our service plan based on two classes of clients: financial planning clients and advisory clients of certain sizes, ranging from $250,000 to $30 million in assets. Obviously, the client who has $30 million requires a little more robust service than the one with $250,000. We analyzed our financial planning process and service delivery down to the level of individual core processes and tasks, which could be integrated into our back office service system. Our service plan ensured the highest levels of consistent service delivery while allowing us to increase our throughput substantially. Every one of our employees must be able to access relevant information about a client, as well as the individual production steps, at any moment. The only way to ensure this happens is to create a powerful database system that puts this information at the fingertips of every employee and establishes a direct link with our clients.

Our goal is to provide clients with an astounding level of service that our competitors cannot easily duplicate. Since institutionalizing our service delivery, we are providing clients with four or five times better service than ever before. Now, we don't compete. We *set* the standards.

I get immense satisfaction from knowing what my organization can provide, without fail, whether I'm making it happen personally or not. And that means that I have personal freedom. I am not the cog in the wheel of my practice. In the future, I can decide to retain my interest in the business and receive a substantial income, whether I am working or not. Or I can decide to sell my equity interest, and because the business does not depend on me to succeed, that equity interest should be worth a pile of money.

 ## BEST IDEA: USE TECHNOLOGY TO ENHANCE SERVICE

You need to develop technological solutions to provide world-class service without fail to every client, every time, no matter who in your organization is providing the service. If your organization can achieve this level of service, you will have few, if any, competitors, and your clients will stay with you forever.

Over the past 20 years, our industry has convinced clients that they need to have an advisor provide comprehensive financial planning and ongoing service. Not many advisors ever really deliver the ongoing service required to ensure clients actually achieve their goals. The use of technology must be maximized in order to deliver a comprehensive and consistent experience for every client.

Technology is a means of support, however, not a substitute, for the expert advisor. Clients—especially seniors who are concerned not only with their own financial needs but also the needs of their children or grandchildren—don't want someone simply to plug their numbers into a sophisticated software program. They want someone to explain things to them, step by step, not because they want to learn to handle their own finances, but because they want to make certain the advisor truly understands their concerns.

TECHNOLOGY SOLUTION   Automated Client Communication and
Event Tracking Program

Communication tracker for

| New Communication | Next Communication | Return to Client Profile |

Communication Date

Type Contact

Call Time

Purpose of Communication

Initials

Notes must include what the client said and what you said.

Open Event Tracker

If an action or an event must be created for this communication, you must create it immediately using the event tracker.

Event tracker for

Event Month

| Previous Event | Next Event | Create New Event | Close Event Form |

Event Frequency

Follow Up Date for the Event

Event Name

Event Assigned to

Event Completed

Event Description

These are the tasks for the

Task Name

Task Assigned to

Task Due Date

Task Started

Task Description

Task Completed

Date Completed

13

Marketing Plan and Sales Strategy

A coherent marketing plan combined with an effective sales strategy is critical to gain and defend market share in today's highly competitive marketplace. Take the time to answer the following questions fully and realistically:

What level of advice and service will you deliver? Initially? Ongoing?

_____

_____

Covering which client financial areas?

_____

_____

What is the sales appeal of your product or service to your target-market?

_____

_____

How will you attract, expand, and maintain your market?

_____

_____

How will you identify and contact prospects? (Advertising, public relations, direct selling, etc.)

_____

_____

How many salespeople will you require? _____

What sales process and materials will they use?

_____

_____

How will you train them?

_____

_____

How will they be compensated?

_____

_____

How will you measure their performance?

_____

_____

What geographic areas will they cover?

_____

_____

What is your product or service pricing strategy? How will it need to change over time?

_____

_____

PROSPECTING

The entire financial services industry has focused almost exclusively on this set of activities. In fact, more effort and resources are focused on developing new clients than on any other part of the business process.

A lot of this activity has centered on getting the client to buy an investment or insurance product. Over the past few years, however, the focus has shifted from product sales to developing a relationship whereby the salesperson becomes the key resource to help clients solve their financial problems and achieve their goals.

If you have been in the planning business for any length of time, you are sitting on a marketing gold mine. Most successful planners have an almost unlimited resource of free prospects. While most other businesses have to spend between 15 and 25 percent of revenue to advertise for new customers, all we have to do is ask our existing satisfied clients for referrals, and we will have more prequalified prospects than we can handle.

This opportunity may not last much longer. As accountants, attorneys, brokers, banks, and insurance companies get into our business, the number of people competing for new prospects will increase dramatically. So act fast. The free prospect sale is going, going, and soon will be gone.

To take advantage of today's opportunity requires that you think outside the box. We actually count client referrals as one of the ways we are compensated. We begin to request referrals as soon as clients have seen the benefit of our work and are satisfied. After they've spent 40 or 50 hours with us, they know that we have their best interests at heart and that we're acting in our fiduciary capacity making quality recommendations for them. We let them know up front that we expect referrals, so they're not surprised when we request them.

We ask every single client to give us five referrals every year. We ask for only the best—people they think we can help the most and who would fit in, as they do, with the type of program we have. We send these referrals a letter saying who is recommending us along with our brochure. Then one of our trained salespeople gives them a call. We don't pressure them; we just tell them we'd like to share some of our ideas with them. As a result, we get more business than we can handle.

If clients don't give us referrals, they can't work with us. That's really strong, but we want to continue to spend 80 to 90 percent of our time working with our existing client base, rather than prospecting. Marketing through referrals is a more cost-effective method of obtaining prequalified prospects and doesn't dilute our energy from servicing existing clientele.

SELLING

Clearly, today's clients want advice and service and place little value on product sales alone. Because planners are limited in the number of clients they can work with effectively, hiring and training new salespeople is extremely important. Success in hiring and training new sales associates is directly linked to your ability to commit your selling process to writing. An institutional sales process is one that can be understood and, therefore, supported by all employees in your company.

When I started in the financial planning business, prospects generally assumed you were either a stockbroker or an insurance agent. They did not understand or believe there really was such a thing as "financial planning." When calling on a new prospect, I found it was really beneficial to have a *sales talk* that explained what financial planning was all about and why we were different from any other financial salesperson with whom they had done business.

We still use pretty much the same sales talk today that we developed almost 20 years ago. Initially, our efforts to train other planners in the use of our sales process met little success, because we failed to put the sales talk and process in writing. Committing the process to writing has enabled us to perfect it, which has also made it easier for new planners to learn and utilize it successfully. In fact, the same sales process that used to take us a year to teach a new sales recruit now takes only three months. So, no matter how you successfully interact with clients, you need to write your method down and create a step-by-step process to instruct others. We break our sales talk down into two distinct phases, each designed to accomplish a specific objective:

1. *Financial planning introduction.* Specifically designed to familiarize prospects with our financial planning process, mission statement, and corporate philosophy.
2. *Sweat tracks.* Involves interviewing the prospect to gather information that will give us a general understanding of the prospect's specific financial situation and allow us to identify potential problems or obstacles to the prospect's success. This phase frequently causes the prospect some discomfort until we show how our firm will resolve the issues.

   At the end of this process, the prospect knows how much retaining our firm will cost and what the benefits will be. They can make a critical value judgment before committing to becoming our client.

We don't work with just anyone. Each client must be a good fit for us. Our sales process allows the planner to determine in the first meeting if we can provide measurable benefits beyond the cost to the client, if the prospect's financial profile meets our target marketing plan, and if the prospect's goals and attitudes "fit," allowing the development of a lasting advisory relationship.

Ask yourself the following questions about your company's sales process:

- Do you have a formal training program for sales associates?
- Do you have a written sales talk?
- Does every salesperson use the same sales talk or process while prospecting for new clients?
- Does every employee understand your sales process?
- How can you make your sales process better?
- How can you enhance your sales process through technology?

The process of training salespeople to become planners is a daunting one. They have to be trained not only to sell, but also to identify solutions to complex financial problems. It takes us about three years to fully train a new salesperson, a significant commitment of corporate resources (not only capital, but also executive time).

How can you justify the risk to your capital and time required to grow your sales team? You need to change the current sales compensation paradigm that exists in our business. Today, most new sales recruits are offered little in the way of salary and benefits. Instead, they are hired as independent contractors and required to build a book of business from scratch, by cold calling prospects. These recruits are lured into the business by offers of high compensation plans—because the new recruit takes all of the risk, he or she is offered the lion's share of the compensation. This level of compensation leaves little, if any, profit incentive for the business owner—incentive required if the owner is to spend the time training the planner in the first place. In addition, cold calling is a precarious enterprise that offers little hope of success and leads to high recruit turnover. This sales and compensation system is actually a legacy inherited from insurance and brokerage companies over the past several decades, and it does not fit the needs of financial planning recruits or business owners.

I happen to believe that part of a business owner's responsibility is to make sure that employees are making their own personal visions come true. If you try to keep all the money for yourself, or you're the only one who gets to take a vacation, you will create resentment among your staff and create competitors from within—

particularly as clients perceive the value is coming from people in your organization, not just you.

I have my key people provide me with their own personal vision statement and update them each year. They, in turn, extend the practice to all employees who report to them. This process is valuable in refocusing strengths and talents. Employees who are achieving their own personal visions have a vested interest in sustaining a world-class business. If your employees are very committed to the success of the company, then you will create measurable and significant shareholder value.

By evolving your business into an institutional quality firm where the value is associated with the firm, not just with one individual, you will also tie in clients, earning more revenue and profit than normally seen with businesses of this type. Then you can really energize your people (as Microsoft has done, for example), by using company stock as currency to compensate and achieve personal financial success for all employees. You'll find this has the effect of creating "golden handcuffs" to help retain key people. You won't have to worry about the competitor down the street, especially the large capital players, luring away the employee who's so well trained by you.

We basically hand clients to new recruits on a platter. Recruits are often surprised at how quickly they can become successful. In our firm, new salespeople concentrate on converting referred prospects into clients and providing relationship management services, effectively coordinating our organizational resources to make sure client goals and needs are met.

In this type of environment, the business owner takes most of the risk, providing training and valuable referrals to salespeople. This new compensation paradigm requires an employment relationship where salespeople receive benefits, salary, and bonuses based on production, but also allows the business owner to keep a large portion of case revenue to compensate for the risks they take.

Because building a referral network takes years, business owners should require salespeople to sign noncompete agreements. Our salespeople are hired to represent our firm, not themselves. New clients are obviously the property of the company, not the sales-person. This principle should be effectively communicated to all new salespeople before they begin employment with your company.

We begin by laying the foundation for success, by providing our salespeople with a uniform sales process. As with everything we do, because the process is in writing, we can use technology to en-hance it.

Because we have institutionalized our sales process, our clos-ing ratio is extremely high, and we have built a sales training pro-gram to transfer the process to new salespeople. Each salesperson must learn our entire sales process, which in turn covers every phase of our financial planning process:

1. Financial Planning Building Blocks Introduction
2. Client Overview Track
3. Estate Planning Track
4. Data Taking Track
5. Plan Presentation Track
6. Implementation Track
7. Relationship Management and Education Track

A key part of the sales process is to appoint a *relationship manager* for each client. This manager acts as a point person for the entire firm, coordinating the rest of the organization's advice and service to make sure that the client's goals can be met.

In addition, we have created three primary avenues for receiv-ing direct input from our clients: first, through the initial financial plan development; second, through in-person client meetings; and third, through the Internet on a 24-hour/7-days-a-week basis. Di-rect input from our clients allows us to learn much more about their preferences and satisfaction level than we could ever learn through traditional marketing research.

This process builds trust and loyalty, differentiating us from the rest of the competition and creating equity in our business. It also turns our clients into our marketing agents; they go out and tell their friends and send us prequalified and pre-endorsed prospects.

It's crucial to find out from your clients if they want, and perceive as value added, what you're providing. You can solicit feedback by developing a questionnaire and providing it to clients via mail on your Web site. In either case, once you have this feedback, you can change or improve your service offerings and establish a strategy to build your brand through *credibility marketing*.

Use credibility marketing to build brand awareness and capture market share. When developing a strategic plan, you need to determine how you are going to get the word out to your target market about your advice and service. The marketing portion of your strategic plan focuses on selling, advertising, and public relations (PR). Credibility marketing is a form of PR that is well suited to the professional financial planner looking to become recognized as the expert in their marketplace.

You can try to implement a PR campaign yourself, or you can outsource to a professional who will coordinate your program. The biggest problem with outsourcing is the cost. Professionals in this area are expensive, but the return on investment can be enormous. Find somebody who's willing to work with you on a retainer basis. We chose outsourcing for two reasons: first, we are not PR experts; second, everyone in our firm already has too many jobs, and to be successful, a PR program must be continuously implemented.

Following is a short outline for setting up a credibility marketing program on your own, but it's not for everyone. If you're content with the status quo, this type of program may be too much work for you; but if you want to earn more—including self-respect and the respect of your clients and your peers—following this program will ensure your success.

Step One—Identify Your Target Market(s)

Begin with a study of your existing clients and develop a deep understanding of their unique needs. As time goes on, expand this to the needs of specific markets you want to serve. The narrower you keep your focus, the better.

Step Two—Know Your Product

You need to know your products inside and out and keep your knowledge up-to-date. Find out how your product can best be used in various situations. *Does your product(s) answer the needs of your target market(s)?*

Step Three—Become a Problem Solver

The trick is to develop solutions to common problems your target market experiences. Make a habit of identifying unique problems your target clients share and of developing creative solutions to solve them. When you become an expert in a market niche, your company becomes invaluable to those clients.

Step Four—Define Your Message

Determine the most compelling message for your particular market niche. The message should indicate your ability to solve problems. You have to communicate the right message to the right people at the right time through the right channels. Does your message address the following:

- What motivates individuals in your target markets?
- What is unique to your product or service?
- What differentiates you from other financial planners, money managers, and financial service providers?
- Why would a prospect choose your firm over the competition?

Step Five—Position Your Company

Positioning is vital to standing out from the hundreds of thousands of financial planning salespeople vying for the same prospects. Think of your company as the product. You want prospects to regard you as a professional with specialized expertise in solving problems in your chosen field. If you position your company correctly as the problem solver and correctly align with market forces, you'll find the door's wide open.

Positioning is the art of controlling perception. David Ogilvy, author of *Confessions of an Advertising Man,* listed 32 important lessons he received during his many years in advertising. He learned that one of the most important actions of all was to correctly position the product (in this case your company). Results, he claimed, were achieved not so much by advertising as by how the product itself was positioned in the marketplace.

Step Six—Communicate Your Message

Get the word out. Discover the most effective way to communicate your company's unique problem-solving capabilities. The secret is to use public relations as a very directed communication strategy.

Local press is great. It provides immediate recognition and feedback. Articles printed in national publications and trade journals communicate that you are considered an expert in your industry. Once your article has been published, leverage it. Call the magazine and ask for reprints of the article, then use these reprints to create a *drip system.* Send reprints to third-party sources, hand them out to clients, and leave them with prospects. Reprints can become your company's calling card of creating instant credibility. They show the world that your company indeed provides a valuable service.

Becoming recognized as an expert creates visibility while building trust and credibility. It can also produce the celebrity effect;

clients and prospects want to be associated with people who are well known. The greater your visibility, the greater your reach, and the more likely people will think of your company's name when they think financial advice.

For more information, read: *The Guide to Financial Public Relations—How to Stand Out in the Midst of Competitive Clutter,* CRC/St. Lucie Press Catalog # JM121, ISBN: 0-910944-12-1, $49.95, by Larry Chambers.

14

Operations and Management Policies and Procedures

Managing a growing organization is challenging, to say the least. However, standardizing your operations procedures will go a long way toward easing the growing pains.

If you want your practice to look and operate like a business, not just a practice, you have to set it up to run like one and engage in the normal functions required of all businesses: marketing, sales, production, purchasing, etc. There is a typical functions chart for a service business on the next page.

Most planning practices are small, spreading all of these functions over a few employees. We often see the owners trying to handle four or five high level functions, which are almost full-time jobs in and of themselves, while still trying to drive sales and service. Earlier, we saw how unmanageable Anne's life had become (see Chapter 3). Her business had grown to the point that all of the executive, sales, and management functions she was trying to carry routinely caused her to work unacceptable hours, seven days a week.

When conducting seminars on the subject of strategic planning, I often ask owners to review the functions chart and write down how many hats they are wearing. I tell them we are going to give the person who wears the most hats a prize. Without fail, we

A Typical Functions Chart

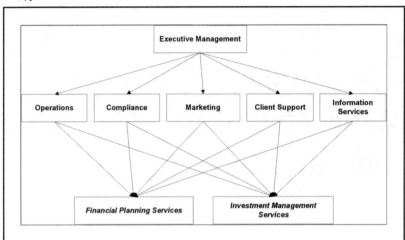

get at least one or two owners who fight for the prize. Guess what the prize is? A dunce cap!

The person who wears the most hats and assumes the most responsibility is not the person who wins, but the one who loses. Like Anne, they can lose what really matters most to them—family, friends, and ultimately their quality of life.

In my personal vision statement, I acknowledge that I want to do the things that make me happy, and I suggest you do the same. If you hate doing something, find somebody else who's really good at it. That person will enjoy a higher level of job satisfaction and so will you. Ask yourself the following questions to make sure you're not wearing too many hats:

Is your business your life?   Yes ☐ No ☐

Who is in control? _____

Are you ready most days to toss the office keys on the desk and walk out?
Yes ☐ No ☐

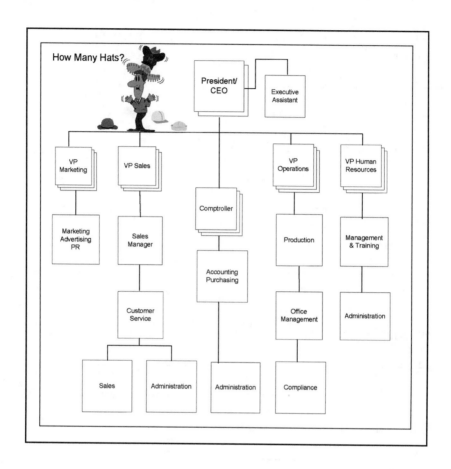

Do you feel as if you're exhausted and personally bankrupt most of the time?
Yes ☐   No ☐

Do you feel that you have little left over at the end of a business day for your family and friends?
Yes ☐   No ☐

Next, try to take a truly global perspective when answering these questions about your organization required to develop policies and procedures:

What are all of the functions you perform in providing clients with services?

_____

_____

How do you manufacture financial plans?

_____

_____

What software is required?

_____

_____

Who inputs client data?

_____

_____

Who reviews the data for completeness?

_____

_____

Who "up curves" the plan, identifying problems and outlining solutions?

_____

_____

Who approves the plan for presentation?

_____

_____

Who is responsible for preparing client documents for implementation?

_____

_____

Once the documentation is signed, who is responsible to make sure everything gets implemented?

_____

_____

What are your administrative policies and procedures for:

Financial Reporting_____

_____

Bookkeeping _____

_____

Billing _____

_____

Accounts Receivable _____

_____

Accounts Payable _____

_____

Purchasing _____

_____

Management Reports _____

_____

Human Resources _____

_____

Employee Training _____

_____

Probation _____

_____

Discipline _____

_____

Compensation _____

_____

Promotion _____

_____

Incentives _____

_____

Bonus _____

_____

Employee Review _____

_____

Annual Reviews _____

_____

Job Descriptions _____

_____

Responsibilities, Duties, and Tasks _____

_____

Development of Standard Operating Procedures _____

_____

What are the functions you provide to your organization that only you can do? Try to distinguish between those activities that only you can do from those you must do because you do not have trained employees capable of accomplishing them.

This is the time to get really honest with yourself. If what you really would like to be doing at work is in conflict with what will make you happy, then the time to change is now.

An accurate appraisal of everything you do is critical to identifying problems and taking corrective action. To accomplish an accurate appraisal, we have developed an analysis tool called the *Responsibilities, Duties, and Task Worksheet* (RDT). The worksheet is broken down by job function and allows you to detail all of the responsibilities, duties, and tasks you perform while at work and the time you take to perform them.

Highlight those tasks that you need to transfer to others. Remember: You should be allocating your energies toward those RDTs that provide your organization with the greatest return and you with the most personal satisfaction.

Build a plan to transfer those RDTs that you don't want to perform. The RDTs that you want to give up form the foundation of your new employee's job description. With a detailed job description in hand, we have found we are much more likely to hire the right person to fit the job.

Be mindful that radical change is dangerous to your organization. Through the strategic planning process, you can develop a model for change that will actually make your organization stronger. Cash flow to support potential pay increases or additional staff should be analyzed carefully. Adequate training time must be integrated into your plan to ensure success. Formalize your RDT by creating a job description for yourself.

RDT   Responsibilities, Duties, and Tasks

		Vice President, Practice	Planning Manager	Bookeeper/Admin Asst.	Operations Specialist	Associate Financial Planner
S Supervisory Responsibility						
R Performance Responsibility						
DT Performance of Duties and Tasks						
RDT Workflow Planning Model		RJC	TD	JK	MC	
Duties	Incumbent	RJC	TD	JK	MC	
I. Overall Practice Management		83%	73%	46%	84%	95%
a. *Miscellaneous*		3%	20%	15%	10%	0%
General oversight and management of financial planning practice		S	S			
Project management - "critical path" scheduling			S		R	
Process client contracts					R, DT	
Process client fees				DT	R, DT	
Rep and corporate licensing			S	DT		
Tracking of commissions to make sure we get paid, and get paid proper amount		S	S	DT		
Advisory fee billing			S	DT	R	
Fee tracking - to be sure we are getting paid by clients			S	DT	DT	
Commission processing		S		DT		
Client filing						
Word processing				DT		
Maintain financial planning software			S		DT	
Staff meetings		S	S, D, T	DT	DT	
b. *New Financial Plan Design and Development*		5%	10%	15%	5%	30%
Coordinate and prioritize practice work flow			S		DT	
Data gathering		S			DT	R, DT
Plan design and development of strategies		S, DT	S,DT			R, DT
Technical research and support						R, DT
Copy client documents				R		
Set up client file				DT		
Factfinder data entry				DT		R, DT
Proof and upcurve client data		S	D	DT		R, DT
Final plan preparation (for production)				DT		R
Plan document production				DT		
Copy plan for files						
Prepare for client meeting - letters, illustrations, spreadsheets, applications, prospectuses		S	DT	DT		R

HUMAN RESOURCES

Human resources issues are every bit as crucial as financial concerns. In a service business like financial planning, the quality of your human capital is much more important than financial considerations. After all, if you don't have the people you need *when* you need them, and if they're not properly trained, then you won't be able to serve your market effectively. Here are some of the human resources issues to consider:

- Do you have the employees you need to accomplish your strategic objective?

- Does each employee know what is expected of him or her?
- Does each employee have a written job description?
- Does each employee know what he or she must do to receive a salary increase?
- Does each employee have regularly scheduled performance reviews?
- Does each employee know what he or she must do to be promoted within the organization?
- Does each employee understand your mission statement, corporate philosophy, and strategic objective?
- Do you communicate the characteristics that define your organization to your employees regularly, empowering them to accomplish your objective?
- Have you determined the level of education and/or training your employees require?

To be successful, on their terms and yours, employees must know what is expected of them, what rewards await them when they meet or exceed these goals, and how they can rise to the next level. For example, at my firm, employees get a raise based on how well they have accomplished certain goals, which are spelled out at the beginning of the performance review period. These goals are based on their job descriptions, personal objectives they've shared with us, and how well they've helped the firm meet its strategic objective. If they meet those goals, they get a raise. If they don't add value, enabling us to achieve our goals, they don't get a raise. It's that simple. And if they don't meet those goals for any lengthy period of time, then they don't work for us anymore, because we must accomplish our objective.

Job descriptions are often ineffectively handled, being too vague on both the individual and corporate level. We have included a Job Description Program in Appendix A to guide you through the detailed process of creating job descriptions. You have to formulate goals for each employee as well as for each department in your organization: sales, finance, advertising, operations, and so on.

At my firm, we draw up a job description for each employee
that includes not only job class (e.g., manager) and salary range,
but also specific goals. How employees think about their jobs, how
they are evaluated, and how they are compensated need to be centered on accomplishing the corporate objective. We embed in each
job description the company's goals, the employee's department's
goals, and the standard operating procedures that he or she will be
expected to follow.

Each of your employees also needs to fill out an RDT. The RDT
allows you and your management team to review what each employee is doing on a daily basis. We have successfully used the worksheet to make promotion decisions and workflow enhancements
and to finalize each person's job description. We also use the RDT
as an integral part of the employee's performance and annual compensation review.

RDT   Responsibilities, Duties, and Tasks Worksheet

Employee:	Don Schrieber, Jr.	Color Code:
Title:	President/CEO	*Responsibilities*
Date:		*Duties*
		Tasks
Activities and Functions Total Allocation	Time Allocated % 100.00%	Can Be Delegated to Whom?
Financial Planning Sales	15.00	
Referral Gathering	3.00	
Cold Calls		
Marketing	2.00	
Minding Clients		
Review Investments		
Plan Presentation	5.00	
Implementation Sales	5.00	

Plan Development	15.00
Data Gathering	5.00
Plan Preparation	
Update Plan Info	
Analysis and Problem Solving	5.00
Analysis and Review of all	
Client Plans	5.00
Financial Advisory—Sales	25.00
Referral Gathering	5.00
Cold Calls	
Marketing	
Minding Clients	10.00
Review Investments	
Plan Presentation	5.00
Implementation Sales	5.00
Plan Development	20.00
Data Gathering	5.00
Plan Preparation	
Update Plan Info	
Analysis and Problem Solving	5.00
Ongoing Consulting	10.00
Business Planning	
& Management	
Consulting Sales	10.00
Referral Gathering	5.00
Cold Calls	
Marketing	
Minding Clients	
Review Investments	
Plan Presentation	5.00
Implementation Sales	
Plan Development	15.00
Data Gathering	5.00
Plan Preparation	3.00
Update Plan Info	3.00
Analysis and Problem Solving	2.00
Ongoing Consulting	2.00

In addition, we have a salary administration policy, something I highly recommend. The salary administration policy describes for all employees where they can go, financially speaking. They know the next step on the ladder and the salary ranges that await them there. No one gets an increase in salary because of tenure; pay is all based on performance. If an employee doesn't earn performance-based increases, then he or she is most likely going to be fired.

The salary administration policy makes the supervisor's job easier, because he or she is guided in the decision-making process. Personally, I hate having to make those decisions. If you hit me on a good day, I want to give you too much money. If you hit me on a bad day, I want to fire you. And you know something? My decision seldom has anything to do with the employee's performance. I know that's really unfair, and that's why we rely on the salary administration policy. (See Appendix C.)

The most valuable asset a company has is its human resources. The company's quality and productivity of the workforce ultimately determines its level of success. Yet all too often we find that more attention is paid to the financial or capital side of the equation during the strategic business planning process. Companies need to determine how they can motivate and channel their human resources to accomplish the company's strategic objective.

Further, you need to determine how to create a positive work environment that will encourage creativity, motivate employees, and provide for goal attainment. After all, the whole idea is to focus all effort and resources to accomplish your organization's strategic objective. In classic business texts, this type of management process is called management by objective. But you need to take this classic concept to the next level—*management by strategic business plan*.

Our formal strategic management process is represented by the following flow chart:

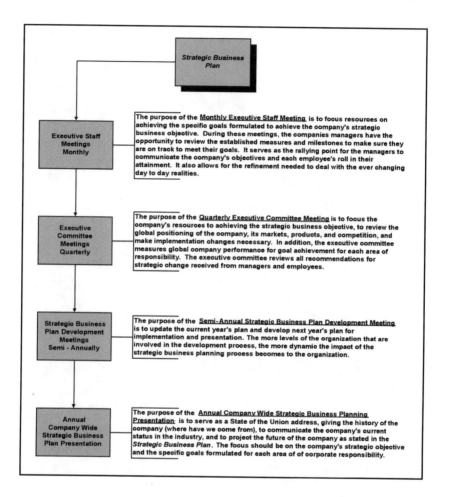

15

Strategic Goals and Milestone Schedule

Your goals determine where you want to go. You can only get there by design, not by default. As you incorporate your personal vision into your strategic business plan, your goals become the driving force in your company. They define all the management functions and determine your needs for people, equipment, and cash flow.

Strategic management, then, is the process of aligning all of the company's resources to accomplish the objective by incorporating the strategic plan into your corporate culture. Each decision you and your management team make during the day needs to be tested against the company's strategic goals and objective.

There is a subtle difference between a company's *mission* and a company's *goal*. A mission is global and described as the company's overall purpose and direction (e.g., "to help affluent clients retain their wealth through effective financial planning and asset management"). In contrast, a goal is specific and normally has a time limit (such as one year or three years) or a particular numerical target (such as increasing sales by 20 percent).

The goals you select usually set off a chain reaction throughout your organization. If one of your goals is to increase your sales, it will probably trigger a need for more people. If your goal is to maximize profit, you may need to cut back on the number of people. If your goal is to expand, you will need more cash to buy more equipment or hire more people.

Here are some guidelines on the goal-setting process:

- *Keep goals clear, simple, and direct.* A common reason that goals are not accomplished is that they're too vague. Whenever possible, make the goal numerically measurable, such as "add ten new clients a month," or "increase assets under management by $5 million a year," and so on. With a measurable goal, employees not only know what they're working toward, but they can chart their progress along the way.

- *Communicate the goals to all employees.* An annual outlook meeting is basically a state-of-the-union address presented by the company's senior managers in which they outline goals for the coming year. This meeting is held in early January for all employees so that they can understand what each unit is expected to accomplish. Shut the organization down for half a day so that everyone can attend. This is one of our most important meetings of the year, because it enables everyone in the organization to see the complete picture.

- *Make sure the goals become a group effort, not just a personal directive.* Your team has to buy into the goals. Unless everyone understands them, accepts them, and commits to achieving them, they have little chance of success. Only through acceptance and commitment by your key managers will you ever meet the goals.

- *Create accountability.* We suggest you have quarterly accountability meetings at which the managers either report that they are on target or, if they are not, work on alternative plans. Each manager also prepares a monthly report comparing actual results to budget projections. Each goal at the corporate, department, and individual employee level should be charted for completion. We recommend the use of Gantt charts to track each strategy and goal to completion.

GANTT CHART Anne's Goal of Hiring a VP of Operations

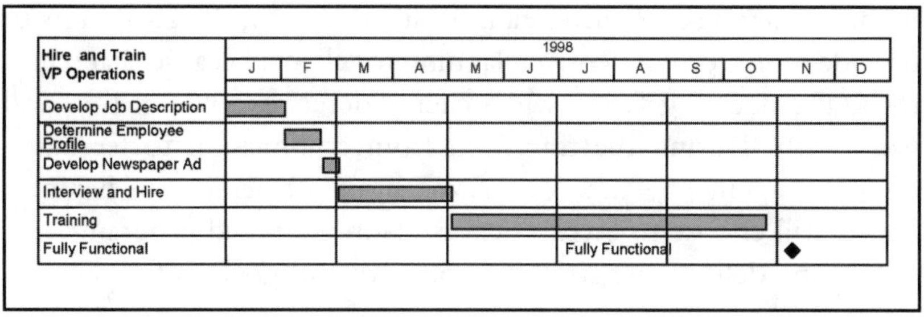
Hire and Train
VP Operations
1998
J
F
M
A
M
J
J
A
S
O
N
D
Develop Job Description
Determine Employee Profile
Develop Newspaper Ad
Interview and Hire
Training
Fully Functional
Fully Functional

Once we have completed a global picture of our organization, industry, and competitors and have finished most of our corporate overview, we are ready to get specific about solving the problems we have uncovered during our planning process.

We previously identified one area of Anne's key problems (see Chapter 3)—her practice has no management infrastructure. She personally provides clients with all material advice and service, and she handles all of the high-level functions in the business. To begin to solve this problem, in addition to hiring a Vice President of Operations and an additional financial planner, Anne needs to develop an alternate sales plan, one which is not dependent on her sales ability to feed her organization.

As part of her business planning, Anne has done a careful analysis of her book of client business. Over the years, she has invested about $60 million for clients in various mutual funds. Recently, she has started to move her clients to fee-based programs and currently has $15 million in fee-based programs. Her firm averages 85 basis points on managed assets, or approximately $107,000.

She has been able to work with about 60 new clients per year, obtained mostly through referrals from existing clients. Until now, Anne looked for an average client to have $250,000 to invest, but she has decided to limit the number of new clients she is going to work with over the next three years, taking only larger clients who have at least $500,000 to invest.

After carefully reviewing the dynamic changes taking place in the industry, Anne decided to accelerate her effort to convert her practice from commission to fees, providing her business with a higher recurring revenue stream. While doing so, she also wants to provide more comprehensive planning for clients because that seems to be the deciding factor when clients determine whom they will work with. During the transition from commission to fee-based asset management, Anne estimates about 50 percent of her new clients will choose to invest their assets in fee-based programs.

Anne defined her strategic objective and goals as follows:

Strategic Objective:

- To change our sales practice into an institutional-quality financial planning company providing financial advice, service, and investment management, which will help clients retire comfortably.
- To broaden the management structure of the organization, providing for corporate continuity for clients and employees while increasing the inherent value of the company.

Organizational Goals:

- Implement and effectively communicate the company's mission statement, corporate philosophy, strategic objective, and strategic plan to employees.
- Establish an equity-sharing plan to attract and retain new key employees by providing them with an incentive to achieve the strategic goals of the company aggressively.
- Develop an employee appraisal and performance system, which will tie employee compensation to strategic goal achievement.
- Institutionalize management processes and service delivery so that all clients perceive value in maintaining a relationship with the company, not the individual planner.
- Develop a sales and training program for new financial planners.

- Develop a training program for the Vice President of Operations.
- Develop a detailed job description for each employee and have each employee develop a set of standard operating procedures covering all aspects of their job.

Sales and Revenue Goals:

- Limit the number of new clients to those with $500,000 or more to invest.
- Contract to provide comprehensive planning with new clients.
- Allocate 50 percent of new assets gathered to fee-based programs.
- Convert $15 million of commission-based assets held by existing clients to fee-based management programs each year.
- Transition rainmaker status to new planners over the next three years, allowing Anne to work part-time.
- Target 50 percent income from recurring streams within three years.

Personal Goals:

After analyzing what is required to solve her current problems, Anne has revised her plan to achieve part-time status over the next 18 months. Anne recognized that she would not be able to hire and train new employees while continuing to produce the level of sales required and move to part-time hours that quickly. She thinks she can accomplish her goals and reduce her workweek over the next year while working a more normal 5-day, 40-hour week. She thinks it is also reasonable to assume she will be able to reduce her week to 4 days the next year and 3 days a week in the following year.

16

Financial Management and Projections

Most business owners view profit as the measure of their success. However, cash flow management is the key to survival.

Whether or not you are ever going to sell your business, you want to build your business *as if* you are going to sell it. Then you are likely to get maximum value out of the business you are building. Focus on creating as much free cash flow as possible to maximize the value of your company.

Profit and cash flow are two entirely different concepts, each with entirely different results. The concept of profit is somewhat narrow, only looking at income and expenses over an entire accounting period. Cash flow, on the other hand, is more dynamic. It is concerned with the movement of money in and out of a business. More importantly, it is concerned with the *time* at which the movement of the money takes place.

You must have financial reporting systems in place to accurately forecast your cash flow. You must also develop good financial controls, allowing you to match expense levels to sales revenue. If not, you are likely to experience periods during which you cannot pay your bills. In the extreme, you might get so far behind that you have to close your business and file for bankruptcy.

Hopefully, you've been creating and maintaining financial records since the inception of your business. If so, most of your work is done. You'll already have balance sheets, income statements, and cash flow budgets for the last three to five years. Your financial reporting systems must be continually upgraded to provide you with the information you need to make critical and timely financial decisions.

We are constantly fine-tuning our financial statements to provide the kind of detailed information that is important to us. Often, we see financial statements that lack sufficient detail to make them a meaningful information source. For example, we break down our income or revenue streams by product or service type. This allows us to keep track of each revenue source to see if we are meeting our targets. There is no sense in fooling yourself with projections that don't match reality. If you consistently project revenue streams that don't match what you have actually accomplished over a trailing three-year period, then you had better revise your projections.

FINANCIAL STATEMENTS   Detailed Information Is a Powerful Tool

	Current	Year to			Current	Year to
Income:	**Month**	**Date**		**Income:**	**Month**	**Date**
Group Commissions				Group Commissions		
Dental				Fee Income		
Life						
Health						
LTD						
401k/Pension			*VS*			
Total Group Comm.						
Fee Income						
Money Management						
Asset Under Discretion						
Assets Under Admin.						
Assets Under Supervision						
Financial Planning						
Initial Plan Fees						
Update Plan Fees						
Total Fee Income						

A useful tip about financial statements: keep them simple and direct with enough detail so that anyone looking at your statements can easily track and understand your company's financial situation. Detailed information is a powerful tool.

Your financial statements are the most objective pieces of evidence that outsiders (lenders and acquirers) will look at either to support or contradict your forecasts of future performance. People have been trained to expect that "history will repeat itself." Make sure your projections are reasonable when viewed against what you have accomplished in the past.

From a practical standpoint, you can base reasonable assumptions on two potential sources of information. If you have an existing business, you have your personal experience on which to rely. Another excellent source is industry groups or associations. You can learn a lot by drawing on the experience of those around you.

You'd be surprised how willing even potential competitors are to share information, if asked in the right way. This is particularly true if your business will serve a limited geographic market and won't directly compete with a similar business located some distance away.

DO YOU KNOW YOUR BREAKEVEN POINT?

The breakeven point for your business is the sales volume you need to achieve to cover all the costs of running your business. It's extremely important for you to know the level of sales required to cover your expenses, and you must have confidence that you can achieve your required sales volume within a reasonable period of time. Otherwise, you need to do more work on the marketing portion of the plan—or to rethink your business idea altogether. Also, recalculating your breakeven point periodically is a good idea, because it will change whenever your overhead costs, pricing structure, or sales volume changes.

If you are not diligent in constructing your financial projections, you can do serious damage to your business and your personal financial situation. When building your financial projections, pay close attention to which costs are fixed or variable. Start by determining all costs of doing business. You may want to use your income statement as an aid.

Variable costs increase directly in proportion to the level of sales in dollars or units sold. Some typical examples would be sales commissions, sales or production bonuses, and wages of part-time or temporary employees.

Fixed costs remain the same, at least in the short term, regardless of your level of sales. Depending on your type of business, some typical examples would be rent, interest on debt, insurance, lease payments and equipment expenses, business licenses, and salaries of permanent full-time workers.

Best Idea—In our business, we have developed a sales tracking system to provide management with detailed information about how much revenue we can expect to receive and when we expect to get it. We track what sales we expect to make over the next several months but that have not been formalized with signed paperwork and a check in hand. Once we have formalized the sale, we change the status from *expected* to *booked*. This allows bookkeeping to collect our accounts receivables. Because the financial planning process usually requires months of work before the sale closes, a tracking system is important to empower the organization to actually capture the business, evaluate sales effectiveness, and ultimately get paid.

One can use many quality accounting programs all available at a low cost and providing basic functions. The one we like and use is *QuickBooks Pro,* a small business accounting package from Intuit. *QuickBooks* is easy to use and supports all of the financial management and reporting requirements of a financial planning or service business. It provides templates that can help you get started quickly. *QuickBooks Pro* provides basic accounting functions such as payroll processing, accounts receivable, accounts payable, invoicing, contact management, job costing and budgeting, time tracking, checking account management and reconciliation, financial reporting, and more.

One of the most beneficial features of *QuickBooks* for a financial planning and advisory firm is the *QuickBooks Timer*. The timer function allows us to keep track of time spent on client service for billing and management tracking. It will load billing information directly into the *QuickBooks* invoicing system, allowing for integrated billing and accounts receivable tracking. We have also found the timer extremely useful to audit each employee's job description. Once or twice a year, each employee audits how he is spending his time over a two-week period. This audit provides management with powerful information on company-wide human resource utilization, allowing us to make better allocation decisions.

If you are still keeping the books for your company, you are limiting your effectiveness as a business builder. This task set is one of the most easily delegated yet pays huge dividends in time, efficiency, and effectiveness. As the leader of your organization, you need to have accurate, timely financial information to make critical decisions. For most small organizations, bookkeeping is not even a full-time job, but data needs to be entered almost daily. Often the data input is let go and the company's financials are a mess. Do yourself a favor and give this job to someone who can do it much better than you can while you concentrate on the big picture—making sure you have the cash flow and financing required to accomplish your strategic goals.

RESOURCES ANALYSIS

The best way to determine if you have adequate resources to accomplish your strategic objective is to perform a corporate resource audit. This audit consists of two parts: a financial resource audit and a human resource audit.

Financial issues to consider include:

What kind of cash flow does the business have? _____

_____

How much cash flow can be reinvested to solve problems and accomplish objectives?

_____

Do you need to raise capital? From a bank? Or do you require funding from other sources?

_____

Have you developed a good relationship with a bank? _____

Do you have the resources available to hire employees or buy new equipment, if needed?

_____

Do you have financial statements for the current year and the past three years?

_____

Develop your financial projections based on fact, not fantasy. Document all assumptions and make sure they work throughout the projection model. Isolate revenue by product or service line. Isolate costs by fixed and variable. Describe any financing required as well as payback terms and schedule. Make sure to analyze the costs associated with growing revenue.

Critical Risks

We all know that financial projections are nothing but forecasts, educated guesses about the future and what we hope to achieve. Unfortunately, in the real world, many factors influence future events. You would not be realistic in the development of your business plan if you did not acknowledge the potential risks that might cause your best laid plans to fail. By addressing these risks in advance, you are more likely to develop effective contingency plans that allow your company not only to survive, but also prosper in difficult times.

- *Prolonged market declines.* Many of the people working in the financial services industry today have never experienced the effects of a prolonged market decline and the problems it can cause. When developing your business plan, you should assess the potential loss of revenue due to client attrition during market declines and try to develop a plan to insulate your business against this loss.
- *Regulatory.* Over the past several years, we have seen sweeping changes in the regulation of investment advisors and brokers who provide financial services to investors. Not only is keeping up with these regulatory changes difficult

for the small advisory firm, so is staying in compliance. Small firms do not have the luxury of dedicated staff with large budgets to interface with compliance attorneys and specialists and stay abreast of the constant changes. Our company and employees are at risk of fine and censure. The only effective solution seems to be to outsource to compliance specialists who will act as our compliance back office.

- *Retention of key employees.* A service business will fail or succeed based on the quality of its human capital. Over the past few years, we have been frustrated by tight labor markets and the lack of qualified workers. Equally frustrating is the challenge of trying to keep talented, highly trained employees from being recruited by larger companies. They lure employees away with up-front bonuses and offers to pay more money than we, as a small company, can ever hope to afford. A potential solution that is working for small businesses all across America is equity sharing with employees. Many employees would like to own a piece of the rock. You can develop equity sharing plans that tie the employee to the company with vesting and by having the employee participate in the accrual of capital through the increasing equity value of your business.

- *Limited capital.* A small business does not have the size, scale, or capital base to compete effectively against the corporate financial giants, banks, brokerages, insurance companies, mutual fund companies, and trust companies. They have the resources to develop fully products and services and market them, while exploiting technology for a competitive advantage. Yet we can leverage our advantages in providing clients with more personal advice and service and niche market opportunities where we are not competing directly with the giants.

A thorough evaluation of the critical risks you face in your business is of paramount importance in developing effective strategies to sustain and prosper over long periods of time in both good and bad markets. The answers to the following questions may be your saving grace later on:

What are the inherent and potential problems, risks, and other negatives your business will/may face?

_____

_____

_____

Is the company or any principal involved in any threatened or pending litigation or disciplinary action?

_____

_____

_____

Is the company facing any stringent regulatory requirements?

_____

_____

_____

Is the company facing legal liability or other insurance problems?

_____

_____

_____

What can you do to avoid these problems?

_____

_____

_____

When are they likely to occur?

_____

_____

_____

How will you deal with them as they arise?

_____

_____

_____

How can you minimize their impact?

_____

_____

_____

What can be learned from these problems?

_____

_____

_____

How can you possibly turn these problems into opportunities?

_____

_____

_____

Through anticipating issues and obstacles, you can consider your options and, perhaps, choose an alternate action or put safeguards into place that will avert or help you recognize potential breakdowns.

18

Strategic Business Plan Appendix and Milestone Evaluation

The appendix section of your plan should include all of the important schedules and information that support your assumptions or provide more detail than included in the body of the plan. Some examples are:

- Historical financial comparisons
- Complete financial projections, with detailed footnotes and assumptions
- Key employee biographical information
- Strategic goals and detailed milestone progress charts

TRACKING YOUR PROGRESS

A well-written plan defines the goals and objectives you wish to achieve over the next few years in specific, quantifiable terms, such as the acquisition of a certain number of clients or any number of other objective measures of success. Whatever the conditions, you'll want to watch your progress toward those goals over time. Your plan will set forth a number of marketing, operational, and financial milestones that will become a useful baseline for tracking and evaluating your actual operating results.

How Frequently Should You Measure?

If you're like me, you're probably going to have a feel for how you're doing because of your involvement with the day-to-day activities. But you still need to use milestones to take a specific performance measure at a particular point in time. You should select your milestones to accommodate two competing considerations. Milestones must occur frequently enough so that you can take appropriate action if you see that interim goals aren't being reached. Take a look each month at certain performance measures that you deem especially important. Waiting until the end of the year, or even the calendar quarter, to check your progress may be too late.

When Things Go According to the Plan

Let's consider the first outcome—basically, that your business is operating the way you'd like to see it. Your performance measurement system is generating data showing that the goals and objectives set forth in your business plan are being met. Congratulations!

Now, make an effort to extend your planning horizon further out in time. Firm up the numbers and fine-tune the plan to get an even better picture. For you, keeping the plan current is easy. Next, and more importantly, begin looking for ways to improve on what you've done so far.

When Things Go Wrong

Despite your best efforts, sometimes a business just doesn't take off the way you expected. An employee may not be performing as you'd like, or estimates contained in the business plan might have been too low. Don't be surprised if you have to address several issues. Some problems will be internal to your business, while others will result from external factors beyond your direct control. In all probability, you won't find just a single root cause.

Following is an example of a way to chart actual results against your expected results for any given month. Once you know the extent of your deviation from what you had hoped to achieve, you can decide what to do about it.

Financial Results (in 1000's)	This Month Actual	This Month Budget	This Month Deviation	Year to Date Actual	Year to Date Budget	Year to Date Deviation	Prior Year to Date Actual
Sales Revenue							
Direct Costs-Sales Comp.							
G&A Costs							
Profit-EBIT							
New Financial Plans Delivered							
New Assets Under Management							

The point is, by checking your progress against milestones, you can make adjustments as you go rather than allocating limited corporate resources improperly.

Institutionalizing Your Business

19

Building an Institutional Quality Business

The whole concept of *practice management* has become a dinosaur in our industry. If you maintain a sales practice business model, you won't be able to compete effectively in the future where larger, supercapital based companies can leverage technology to reduce fees while providing more service. Building a world-class financial planning business that will sustain itself in the future requires streamlining your operations in response to competitive pressures. Institutionalizing your systems will allow you to continue to provide a level of client-specific, customized advice and service at a competitive fee.

When you offer a service level that's world-class and cannot be replicated easily by competitors, you have no competitors. You can charge whatever the market will bear. You can offer full spectrum financial planning that CPAs, attorneys, and insurance agents are not really capable of providing and that isn't available on the Internet today. You can grow an organization large enough in size and scope to be able to compete with the institutional-quality services the large financial conglomerates deliver.

First and foremost, you must stop operating your company by the seat of your pants and adopt a management process that goes beyond managing by objective to *managing by strategic plan*. Each decision you and your management team make during the day needs to be tested against the company's plan—its strategic goals and objective. The focus of your entire organization will shift from day-to-day crisis management to fulfilling your corporate mission by implementing the strategic plan you have created.

As with everything in business, a plan works best when it has been formalized and tested through trial and error. Let's take a look at the process we use to bring our strategic plan to life in our organization.

COMMUNICATION

Communicating and reinforcing your company's mission, philosophy, strategic objectives, and goals is the responsibility of not only the owners but also each of the executives, managers, and employees. If the owners are the only ones who care about the plan, then you will accomplish nothing.

Our communication plan has two parts: *formalized meetings* and *human resource management integration*. But, before we review our meeting process, you need to know that *I hate meetings*. We just don't have much time to allocate to sitting in meetings. All of our employees have more than full-time jobs, and everyone is acutely aware that each meeting costs productivity. With that said, I can also assure you that without formally setting aside time to communicate your business plan, the plan will die and along with it, your hopes of institutionalizing your business.

Because meetings seem to be a necessary evil, we have developed some rules to make sure our meetings are productive and effective:

- Every meeting must have a formal agenda
  - circulated at least two days in advance for additions or deletions.
  - detailing any information required to be reviewed before the meeting.

- Formal minutes must be taken and must
  - detail what was discussed.
  - specify who is responsible for each task or project.
  - list the expected completion date for each task or project.
  - circulate within three days after the meeting for edits and approval.
- Agenda and minutes should be formatted to include old business and new business.
- Adopt formal meeting procedures (we use a simplified version of Robert's Rules of Order to ensure smooth meeting operations).
- Time management for meetings is crucial.
- Specify the length of your meeting.
- Start and end your meetings on time.

Attendees are accountable for meeting participation. They need to come to the meeting prepared, having worked between meetings to accomplish their assigned tasks and to move their project to the next phase.

It helps to have a dedicated resource in your company not only to manage the meeting information flow but also to act as a facilitator for task and project management between meetings. Depending on the number of meetings and projects outstanding, you may need to designate an employee to act as a resource for members to assist them in accomplishing their assignments. In our company, the president's executive assistant fills this key meeting resource.

Formal Meetings

We use the following formal meetings outline to communicate and reinforce the company's strategic objectives and goals and to update the strategic plan:

Formal Meetings Outline

Executive Strategic Plan Update

Purpose:
- To review and update the strategic business plan.
- To focus on the global business environment and strategic planning required to achieve the company's strategic objectives.

Frequency of meetings: Semiannual, offsite meeting with eight-hour duration

Executive Committee

Purpose:
- To review status of implementation of the company's strategic business plan, focusing on attainment of strategic objective, strategic goals, and milestone measurement.
- To review strategy and resolve problems blocking goal attainment on a global level.

Frequency of meetings: Quarterly on Thursday, 12:00 (Lunch)

Executive Staff

Purpose:
- To focus on operating issues as they relate to strategic plan implementation, leading to a detailed problem-solving approach to operating implementation of the plan.

Frequency of meetings: Monthly on a Thursday, 12:00 (Lunch), duration of two hours. (Except once per quarter when ECM meets.)

Planning Operations

Purpose:
- To focus senior planning staff on planning practice issues required for task assignment, workflow planning, and priority conflict resolution.

Frequency of meetings: Weekly on Thursday, 10:00 AM

Investment Management Operations

Purpose:
- To discuss operational issues affecting Operations, including resource management and project tracking.

Frequency of meetings: Monthly on Thursday, 11:00 AM

Corporate Operations

Purpose:
- To discuss general company operations including equipment, facilities, and human resource management issues.
- To track and prioritize projects to completion.

Frequency of meetings: Biweekly on Thursday, 9:00 AM

Strategic Plan Presentation

Purpose:
- To present Strategic Business Plan to all employees, updating them on goals and objectives and to measure our performance as a company.

Attendees: All employees

Frequency of meetings: Semiannual, January & July, offsite, eight-hour duration

Communicate Your Business Plan

To succeed in implementing your business plan, each and every employee in your firm must adopt the plan. We start each year with a Strategic Plan Presentation meeting, where we share how well we accomplished last year's goals and outline the goals we have set for the coming year. We generate a lot of excitement at this meeting. Employees get charged up because they feel they have an integral role in accomplishing the goals we have set down.

While this meeting sets the tone for the coming year, the excitement we create wanes quickly unless we continually communicate and reinforce the strategy and goals with the employees. Each executive and manager is encouraged to share, at least monthly, how they and the employees who report to them are achieving their assigned goals.

KEYS TO INFRASTRUCTURE AND STAFFING PLANNING

To institutionalize your business you need to analyze your business in detail, dissecting your business model to determine the key functions you and your employees are required to undertake during your day-to-day work lives. We have found that our business, a typical wealth management company, can be separated into three functional business units, each providing integrated support and services to each other and to our clients.

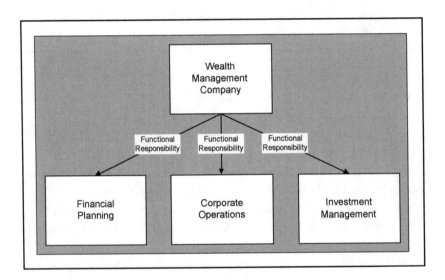

Corporate Operations

Corporate Operations is the backbone of any going concern where the seemingly routine, yet critical tasks of running a business are concentrated. Core functions in our company that we identify as essential functions include:

- Financial management (forecasting, bookkeeping, purchasing)
- Compliance (licensing, continuing education, regulatory)
- Human resources (benefits, employment practices, employee performance evaluation and reviews)
- Information services and technology (technology planning, network design and administration, software evaluation and development)
- Marketing (advertising, public relations, brand development, sales process development)

Financial Planning Firm Functions Chart

Financial Planning Firm Functions Chart

Operations | Compliance | Marketing | Client Support | Information Services

Financial Planning | Investment Management

In developing your business plan you need to carefully analyze each of these core functions of corporate operations to determine who in your organization is best suited to be responsible for plan coordination, supervision, and implementation in each area. Part of empowering your organization to grow, to become a self-sustaining entity, is to delegate these important functions to your staff. In a sales practice, many of these function are the responsibility of the owners, who also have the key responsibility to generate revenue to sustain the organization. Obviously, this is just more of the same "cog in the wheel" syndrome so common in our industry.

Each of these functions is critical to a company's ability to survive and grow, but most sales practice owners regularly ignore these areas, only paying attention when a problem arises. We focus on these areas as we develop our business plan; it is here where we decide who will be responsible for each function. As with any small growing organization, we often find a mismatch between the number of functions to be assigned and the number of people to delegate to. The strategic planning process allows us to identify potential workflow overloads and plan staffing accordingly. (This is the benefit of having an integrated human resources platform with workflow planning tools like the RDT worksheet and written job descriptions.)

As our business grows, we pay strict attention to the level of staffing required to support our business model. Our staffing models not only include our current staff positions, but they also identify positions that we will need to add within the next 24 months and integrate those staffing needs into our cash flow planning and budgeting.

While this staffing chart may look unrealistic for many small planning practices, the purpose is to recognize the need to plan for

Corporate Operations Staffing Chart

Corporate Operations

President/CEO

- Vice President Operations
- Director Operations
- Operations Manager
- Compliance Manager
- Operation Specialist
- Operations Assistant
- Administrative Staff

staff additions as your business grows. Growth creates a heightened need for all key business functions to be accomplished, and the stress on your employees can be overwhelming, leading to burn-out, demoralization, and eventually high, even chronic employee turnover. You can find many examples of this type of stress in your business if you are willing to look. In our case, we recently felt a tremendous strain in supervising our compliance function. In the past a few key salespeople were generating all of our revenue, but several years ago we initiated an organic growth strategy to signifi-cantly build our sales force. We found it is one thing for the own-ers in our company to be comfortable with sales compliance, when in essence we were supervising ourselves, but a completely differ-ent matter to be on the compliance hook for a hoard of new sales-people. We needed to completely revamp our compliance and sales supervision systems. However, we did not have a single employee in our firm with the excess capacity to assume responsibility for this key function. Our first step in developing a staffing solution was to outsource most of our new compliance initiative to a firm that spe-cializes in compliance. Our next step, which will be implemented within the next two years, is to hire an experienced compliance man-ager as part of our corporate operations support team.

Your staffing plan should coordinate the key functions that you need to accomplish across your entire business model. We have found that it was much easier to do this type of planning after we had analyzed our business functions, so we could split our business into business units reflecting our core product and service offerings (i.e., financial planning and investment management).

Financial Planning Division

Our financial planning business unit's focus is to provide our clients with the highest level of client-specific comprehensive plan-ning and turnkey financial management available. The following staffing chart reflects the staff levels required to cover all of the functions covered by our planning business unit.

Financial Planning Staffing Chart

Financial Planning Division

Vice President - Planning

- Director of Planning
- Sales Manager
- Senior Planner
- Planning Manager
- Associate Planner
- Planning Specialist
- Operations Specialist
- Administrative Staff

We segregate the key functions in our planning division into the functions and activities related to finding and converting prospects into clients (sales), and those minding and grinding functions such as plan manufacturing and ongoing client service. This helps us more effectively plan for staff additions, because it becomes easy to see the relationship between adding new sales associates, who will drive client acquisition, and the associated increase in activity required in plan manufacturing and ongoing client service.

Investment Management Division

We started our investment management division in 1990 to provide investment management to our clients on a fee basis, rather than the commission-driven system that we had used up to that point. We undertook significant planning before starting our fee-based initiative. One of our goals in creating our money manage-

Planning Division Key Functions

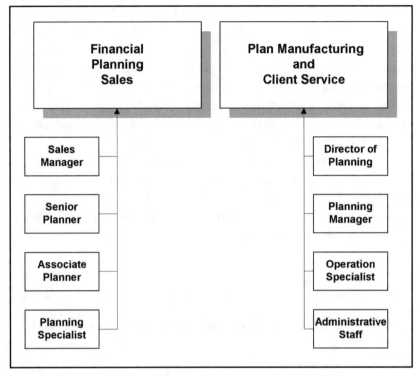

ment process was to provide our clients with an investment pro-gram designed to solve for each client's required rate of return, while giving each an investment experience within his or her spe-cific risk tolerance. We designed our investment program to pro-vide our financial planners with an investment solution that meets clients' specific rate of return requirements, while taking into ac-count their feelings about volatility and risk. From the beginning we knew that we would be unable to provide a client with an invest-ment process that would deliver significant value if we attempted to build and manage money on a part-time basis. Our strategy was to build a separate investment management division that was truly in-stitutional in quality, to not only manage our clients' money, but to also manage other advisors' clients' money as well. We knew before we started that we lacked the investment capital or cash flow to simply build the required staff to manage money effectively; our total first year budget was only $100,000. We had to find a better way. As luck would have it, we had the executive experience and talent to not only manage money, but the programming capability to build an extremely efficient management process based on leveraging technology rather than hiring people. But, as with any growing business, we have found that technology can only take you so far; you need people to implement your process.

We also break the investment management division's core functions down into two areas: portfolio management and operations. The staffing chart below details the staffing assignments that we have determined are necessary to build world-class investment management products and services.

Investment Management Staffing Chart

Investment Management Division

Vice President - Investment Management

- Portfolio Manager
- Operations Manager
- Trader/Research
- Operations Supervisor
- Operation Specialist
- Operations Assistant
- Administrative Staff

To review, as part of the process of institutionalizing your business you will need to

- completely analyze all of the functions you have to perform in your organization.
- separate your business into units defined by the products and services you offer.
- build an integrated staffing model to assist in workflow planning.
- integrate planned staffing additions into your cash flow planning and budgeting.

Performance Measurement

In many companies, the business plan never seems to come to life but only receives lip service from the executive suite several times a year. If you want your employees actually to buy into the plan, their job performance must be tied to specific strategic goal accomplishment. We integrate the company's strategic goals right into their job descriptions.

We update and review their job descriptions and performance targets with them formally at least once per year. In addition, each manager updates his team on milestones and goal accomplishments at least once a month. Through ongoing communication, employees can measure if they are on track to achieve their performance targets, and if not, they can make required adjustments. An interesting side effect can arise as employees actually push each other, their managers, or the executives to increase performance to meet the company's goals.

To be competitive, every small company needs to create the most productive work force possible. By using appraisal standards that are objective and measurable, you ensure that managers will recognize and reward employees for skills that further the goals and profits of the company. Annual and semiannual performance appraisals form the basis of determining if employees are meeting or exceeding the goals set in their job descriptions for the purpose of important promotion and salary decisions. When employees believe they are judged fairly, they will respect the system and view appraisals as a way to improve their performance. (See Appendix B for Performance Appraisal Kit.)

Updating Your Business Plan

Every business, large or small, needs to re-create itself from time to time. Large corporations call this process reengineering. Business planning is a dynamic process that needs to be continually updated to reflect changing economic and industry conditions, as well as any changes in your personal vision.

For instance, I have a significant desire to build a much larger organization. I can see my vision for the business really coming together. In this vision, my company has a national infrastructure, hundreds of employees, and a dominant position as one of the best financial advisory companies in the industry.

One of the problems I have with this vision for a larger business is that it may be in direct conflict with my personal vision for my life. The most important thing in my life is to make sure that I'm a good husband and father. Trying to build a national infrastructure with limited resources would probably mean I'd have to sacrifice my family. So, I won't do that.

My personal vision statement:

- I don't want to be the cog in the wheel.
- I don't want to be the only person in my firm giving advice and service.
- I want my life to be manageable.
- I want to make sure that our clients get the highest quality service and advice—they're entitled to it.
- I want to make sure that I don't sacrifice my family in doing that.

These things are the most important for me. They become the anchor of why we're implementing this strategic business planning process and making changes in the company. I keep my personal vision statement on my desk right in front of me as I help my clients achieve their goals.

If you are like me, you will have to revisit and test every part of your business plan against your personal vision to make sure your business facilitates accomplishing *your* personal goals.

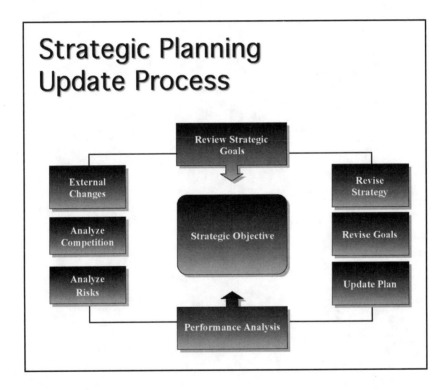

Strategic Planning Update Process

- Review Strategic Goals
- External Changes
- Analyze Competition
- Analyze Risks
- Strategic Objective
- Revise Strategy
- Revise Goals
- Update Plan
- Performance Analysis

20

Uniformity and Standardization

As planners become successful in the business, they all get to the same threshold where they have more clients than they can service, yet too few to become really successful. And, as we discussed earlier, they compound this problem by channeling all client services and advice through one person, themselves *(Mistake #1)*. Their clients and, therefore, potential acquirers, perceive little value in the rest of the organization.

With the advent of large financial conglomerates competing for clients, growing your business beyond the one-planner or two-planner practice typically found in our industry becomes critical. To grow may require reengineering your business model, then institutionalizing its processes. Every function, activity, and task that employees undertake each day need to be formalized into standard operating procedures (SOPs).

The SOPs will foster success rapidly throughout your organization day-in and day-out by providing a consistently high level of service to current clients. They will also have the added benefit of changing the client's perception of who is providing them with service, transferring much of the focus from the individual financial planner to the entire organization, thereby allowing the planner to focus on new client acquisition.

The dilemma for most planners is determining where to start the reengineering process. Some years ago, the planners in our company were working too hard, and each new client made the situation more unbearable. Our reengineering process started with a desire to solve a problem common to all financial planners: *a limited amount of face-to-face time to spend with each client.*

The breakthrough for us was to identify what we actually did each day in our business and then to break each function down into specific activities, each activity into tasks, and each task down into procedures. Over the past five years, we have dissected every operation, process, and procedure to determine the best model or methodology to accomplish our strategic objective. We discovered that we performed one primary function—*planning*—which can be broken down into three basic activities: *finding, minding,* and *grinding.*

Finding activities take place in the front office, *minding* activities represent the middle office, and *grinding* activities are the back office of our business. This delineation of the front office (sales), middle office (relationship management), and back office (service) is crucial to institutionalizing your business. The functions and activities need to be supported by employees who specialize in these diverse functions.

FINDING

Much of what the financial planner does encompasses activities required to find clients, most often referred to as the sales process. For most planners, the sales process includes *identifying* their potential client (target marketing), *prospecting,* and then *selling* these prospects on the benefits of doing business with this planner. In other words, the financial planner converts prospects into clients.

Knowing who your ideal prospect is really is important. Then you can tailor your product and sales message to fit the needs of your target market. Most small business owners fail to develop a thorough marketing plan, and they fall prey to *Mistake #6:* Not knowing who or how large your target market is.

You need to take the time to do some research. We have, and we've found that seniors control two-thirds of the wealth in the United States. How do you get these people as clients? You find out what they want and design your business to provide them with exactly what they want. Even though the senior market is huge—35 million—you've got a lot of competition, right? After all, everyone these days seems to be calling themselves a financial planner: accountants, insurance agents, stockbrokers, bank executives, and so on. In reality, though, only about 20,000 financial professionals in the United States offer comprehensive planning services to their clients—the services seniors are looking for. Speaking in very general terms, that works out to about 1,750 seniors for each practicing financial planner, more than enough for each planner to build a very successful business but way too many to handle in a traditional financial planning practice.

No way can you effectively serve even half that many people if all the advice and service is being channeled through one or two people. However, by institutionalizing your sales and management process, you can design systems that allow each salesperson to increase the number of clients he or she can serve. To accomplish this, you must create specialized sales support teams that will allow the planner to concentrate on sales and relationship management, while other employees provide the balance of services and support to the planner as well as the client.

Practice management pundits often disagree on the optimum planner-to-client ratio. Some seem to think that planners should concentrate their efforts on working with 25 large clients, while others say the optimum number is somewhere between 50 and 100 affluent clients. The optimum really depends on many factors: the number of hours the planner wants to work, the type and complexity of services offered, the size and complexity of the clients the planner works with, and so on.

Even after you have developed a world-class service organization with empowering technology, your planners will be hard pressed to provide comprehensive services to more than 100 clients. A planner can only spend so much face-to-face time with clients.

Once the planner reaches the client saturation point, the quality of advice and service begins to decline—a situation with devastating consequences for your practice, unless you've taken steps to institutionalize *relationship management.*

MINDING

The most important activities (and the ones that will determine the long-term success of your business) are the *minding* or relationship-management functions performed by the people in your organization. These encompass making sure that the relationship with the client is secure and that the client's needs are being met. From complex, advice-giving activities to the more mundane service calls, each minding activity must be handled in a manner that enriches the client relationship and reinforces their desire to continue to work with your organization. Relationship management and top-quality service are the keys to building a competitive advantage for your business.

Financial planning solutions can often make a client's financial situation more complex. Most clients don't want to handle the complexity of their current financial situation, which is why they seek outside help, much less one that is made more complex through the planning process. The thought of their situation becoming more complex is exactly opposite of what they are looking for, so the middle and back-office functions of your business are critical to keeping these clients.

Why all this focus on keeping clients? Because satisfying clients leads to high client retention. High client retention leads to high recurring revenue. High recurring revenue leads to very predictable levels of revenue and profit, which leads to very high equity value.

Our whole industry, the financial services industry, has always been focused on client acquisition, not on client retention. And because we've moved to the fee-based model, it's startling to me that people haven't figured out that we're really in the client-retention business now, not the client acquisition business. You have to acquire new clients to continue to grow, but keeping existing clients happy is much more important.

Existing clients should be where new clients come from. If they are the key component of your marketing plan because they are your referral source, then that's all the more reason why you must keep them happy. The most successful managers and financial advisors have an endemic marketing machine that doesn't really cost them anything—if they'd just pay attention to their clients. There's got to be a reason why the client refers people to you. It's not a natural process; it's one that causes clients a great deal of concern.

Clients worry about how the prospect will react to the referral and whether harm will come to any of the relationships involved (the planner-client relationship, the client-prospect relationship, or both). So the client incurs some risk personally, and he or she must have a very compelling reason to go out on a limb and refer you to friends and colleagues. How can you alleviate that risk? By offering tremendous service: your clients feel that there just couldn't be a better advisor than the one they're doing business with.

Institutionalizing the minding process—creating a uniform service platform so that clients always receive a consistent high level of service regardless of which employee addresses their particular need on a particular day—is not just for keeping in touch with clients. It's keeping track of their needs.

In order to enhance service and throughput, we have broken functions down into three areas: planning, investment management, and operations. We created job specialists in each area. For example, the planning specialist job description is as follows:

Job Description and Performance Goals

Title: WBP Planning Specialist
Job Class: 3C
Salary Range: $35,000–$45,000

Position Summary: This position reports to Planning Manager–WBP. The primary responsibilities of this position are to maintain rela-

(continued)

tionships with new and existing clients by providing support and service in accordance with Wealth Builders's client service plan, and to assist in the development of new and updated financial plans in accordance with the Wealth Builders's plan development process. The major areas of responsibility for this position and their intended results include (in order of priority):

I. Maintain, nurture, and enhance existing client relationships through support and satisfaction of client requests for service. Advance the implementation of the WBP Client Service Plan so as to set Wealth Builders, Inc. and its employees apart from the competition, and change the focus of service from the individual planner to Wealth Builders as a company, thereby adding value in our client relationships.

II. Provide sales support to Senior and/or Associate Financial Planners before, during, and after financial planning meetings, to gather and verify data and to develop relationships with clients.

III. Serve as primary relationship contact for clients with regard to maintaining and furthering the relationship. Responsible for the resolution or delivery of requested service or service commitment as outlined in the WBP Service Delivery platform.

IV. Performance of all job responsibilities, duties, and tasks so as to contribute to the attainment of revenue and profit goals of the Wealth Builders, Inc. Strategic Business Plan, while maintaining our high standard for quality.

Primary Duties

Your primary duties as they pertain to this position will be as follows:

1. Ongoing client support and service in accordance with Wealth Builders, Inc. specified client service plan, including:

   a. Perform "minding" of client relationships by handling client calls and responding to client requests for service where necessary, coordination with other Wealth Builders, Inc. personnel to provide value-added problem solving and service.

   b. Implement service consistent with established client profiles according to Wealth Builders's service plan.

   c. Provide assistance in coordination and completion of financial plan updates, investment reviews, tax reviews, and other services as required.

   d. Track tasks and communicate priorities for above items with WBP staff consistent with direction from Senior Planner and Planning Manager.

2. Design and development of financial plans in accordance with the Wealth Builders's plan development process checklist, with duties to include:
   a. Perform technical research and support where required.
   b. Prepare plan presentation package, including implementation summary and estate plan models.
   c. Coordinate planning practice staff to effect efficient implementation of recommendations.
   d. Communicate with client during implementation of recommendations.
   e. Perform special projects.
   f. Provide ongoing client service.
   g. Plan item implementation.
3. Preparation for client meetings:
   a. Schedule and confirm appointments.
   b. Work with Senior Planner to determine what is needed for meetings and coordinate with WBP staff to prepare for meetings.
   c. Debrief with Senior Planner following client meetings to determine service requirements and follow up.
4. Coordination and follow up on insurance underwriting:
   a. Work with underwriting groups to streamline and expedite insurance underwriting.
   b. Communicate status to clients.
5. Monitoring both input and output for income/transaction database:
   a. Obtain information from Senior Planner following client meetings.
   b. Complete input sheets.
6. Develop and follow through on training and education plans:
   a. Wealth Builders, Inc.—client service and client management training.
   b. Wealth Builders, Inc.—financial planning education and technical training.
   c. Wealth Builders, Inc.—sales training program.

This Job Description is intended to indicate the general nature of the work to be performed and is not to be interpreted as a comprehensive inventory of all the responsibilities and duties required of employees assigned to this position. The nature of our business requires all employees, from time to time, to perform tasks that are not necessarily associated with a particular job description.

Uniform Service Platform

About six years ago, we were faced with choosing between sacrificing service to existing clients who had helped us build our business, or limiting the growth of our firm by declining to take on new clients. Both alternatives were unacceptable, and we knew we had to find a better way.

We compared the revenue generated from new clients versus the endemic and recurring revenue from existing clients. Because 80 percent or more of our revenue came from existing clients, we realized that if we lost clients because we sacrificed service to look for new clients, we'd be at much greater risk to our business model than if we didn't get any new clients.

Our average new client generated only about $17,000 in revenue in the first year. But this same client would generate $185,000 in revenue over a 10-year period ($18,500 per year), and $425,000 to the firm over a 20-year period ($21,250 per year).

Obviously, client retention was much more important to our long-term profitability and success than acquiring new clients.

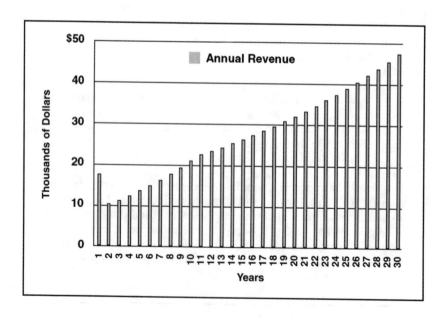

We determined that we needed to design systems to ensure that every one of our clients received the highest level of service, thus reinforcing their need and desire to continue to work with our organization. Additionally, we could effectively serve more clients. This conclusion led us to develop our *uniform client service platform.*

But how do you create a uniform service platform when you provide clients with customized financial planning? Because face-to-face contact is the limiting factor for all of us and ultimately determines the number of clients each planner can work with, we solved this dilemma by recognizing that while each client's situation and goals differ, the level of advice and service that we need to provide is dependent on the size and complexity of their financial situation. We analyzed our clients by income, net worth, invested assets, and job situation to determine the minimum level of service required by each client, then grouped them with clients with similar service needs.

Because our core offering centers around providing financial planning, we started with the need to update a client's financial plan. To add value as planners, we need to look at each client's situation with fresh eyes and updated data to determine if they're on track to achieve their goals, given current economic and investment conditions as well as the tax environment. We determined that each client, regardless of size or circumstance, needed to participate in formally updating his or her financial plan annually.

Next, we determined the number of face-to-face investment review and client education meetings we needed to conduct with each client. We found this was dependent on the size and complexity of the client's investment holdings and income tax profile, so we grouped clients accordingly. The larger and more complex a client situation, the greater the need for client contact. Client contact can take many forms: face-to-face meetings, e-mail, direct mail, telephone, Web site, etc. We have built each type of communication into our client service platform to mind the client relationship properly. To be successful, we determined that we needed to contact our clients an absolute minimum of 12 times a year.

I'd say that, between the contact that we initiate with the client and contact that the client initiates with us, we would actually touch base with our standard $500,000 client about 20 times a year. Someone from our organization is minding that relationship on a consistent basis.

Today, we have established six uniform service levels that we assign to clients according to their financial profile. We then customize a client's uniform service profile with other service modules to provide for each client's unique needs. For instance, we have three service levels for our planning clients: Silver, Gold, and Platinum.

Silver Planning Service Level

Silver Planning Client Profile	Minimum	Service Provided	Frequency
Income	$ 100,000	Comprehensive Financial Plan	Annually
Net Worth	1,000,000	Implementation Service	Ongoing
Total Investment Assets	500,000	Investment Reports	Quarterly
WBI Managed Assets	250,000	In-Person Investment Review	Semi-annually
		Tax Review	Annually

Each investment management client receives performance reports and a quarterly newsletter. We also provide tax updates. Usually at least once a year, we provide information to the client and their accountant. (We don't offer accounting services right now, although we will in the future.) The accountant gets all the client's tax information; as the client's account size grows larger and their asset base more complex, we increase reporting to quarterly. We make sure that everybody on the advisory team has up-to-date information and is on track to help the client achieve their goals. As a client's financial assets increase, so does the complexity of their financial situation. We make sure not only to integrate more service and higher levels of advice but also to provide more face-to-face interaction.

We provide advisory clients with a higher level of service not only through our back office but also on a face-to-face basis, because their more complex situations demand it. They're wealthier, or they're business owners. The client with $10 million or more invested sees us every month, and we provide their accountants with quarterly tax reviews.

Silver Advisory Service Level

Silver Advisory Client Profile	Minimum	Service Provided	Frequency
Income	$ 500,000	Comprehensive Financial Plan	Annually
Net Worth	5,000,000	Implementation Service	Ongoing
Total Investment Assets	2,500,000	Investment Reports	Quarterly
WBI Managed Assets	1,000,001	In-Person Investment Review	Quarterly
		Tax Review	Semi-annually

Our goal is to bring family office services—services that a wealthy family would go out and hire a team of 20 to 200 people to accomplish—to merely affluent clients. Traditional family offices have their own accountants, attorneys, trust officers, investment managers—everything. Not long ago, you had to have about $100 million in order to get that level of service. Today, technology enables us to offer family office services to clients with $1 million in assets.

A key part of this process is appointing a *relationship manager* for each client. The relationship manager acts as a point person for the entire firm, coordinating the rest of the organization's advice and service to make sure that the client's goals can be met. All employees must be responsible for client relationship management, but the planner and planning specialist are directly responsible in our organization for *minding* each client relationship. It is a key focus of their job descriptions, their annual evaluations, and compensation treatment.

This is all part of institutionalizing the management process and the relationship with the client to deliver high-quality service consistently. You must create standard operating procedures for everything your firm offers, and everyone in your organization must follow these procedures at all times. Doing so can eliminate a lot of confusion and avoid providing less than stellar client services.

Let me give you an example. Over the years, we've worked with attorneys to help clients establish estate plans. One popular strategy that really used to create problems was when the client requested an irrevocable trust that included life insurance.

As you know, clients establish such trusts so that the insurance benefits are excluded from their estate when they die. Often a family member is named as trustee, and he or she has certain obligations regarding Crummey notices; that is, notifying the beneficiaries each year that they have the right to withdraw premium payments rather than maintaining the policy. Now, many trustees do not understand their obligations in this regard, and the insurance agent who sold the policy and the attorney who helped draft these trust documents rarely take it upon themselves to follow up each year.

Because the client, the trustees, and the beneficiaries need someone to provide annual assistance, clearly we could add value in this area. We added a complete trust management module to our service platform that allows us to send the client a notice of premium before the insurance company does. The client's deposit is in the trust for the 30 days or more that it's required to be there, in the trust checking account. We also send out the Crummey notices and make sure they're returned, then add them to the client data file. In short, we offer complete turnkey trust management.

Today, a client with an irrevocable trust doesn't have to worry about anything. We've eliminated a nightmare for them. Do you think this client will ever leave our firm? Of course not. Our key to success is to offer a level of service our competitors cannot match. (In fact, many of them don't even think along these lines.)

Similarly, we have a whole module that does complete minimum distribution management for clients. Clients often have multiple custodians for retirement accounts, and the planner is the only person who knows where all those accounts are. Schwab will do minimum distribution calculations on the money it has, and Merrill will do it on the money it has; but minimum distribution rules require you to aggregate all IRA or qualified accounts, get the 12/31 value, and then determine what your minimum distribution is. If it's calculated incorrectly, the client has tax problems, interest and penalties. If the client forgets to make withdrawals, the penalties are huge. Relying on someone to handle these concerns gives the client peace of mind.

These are just a few examples of the hundreds of service tasks that must be accomplished to make sure that the client's needs and goals are met. We provide turnkey financial advice and management, but we also provide a personal relationship.

Institutionalizing the relationship management process allows us to provide a high level of personal service that involves the whole firm. Clients benefit by knowing that many of their questions or concerns can be addressed by anyone in the organization, not just their designated planner, and the firm benefits because a lot of the relationship management responsibility is transferred from the planner to the staff. Clients learn that if they want to know if their tax reports went out, they shouldn't call the planner. He has no idea; that's not his job. Instead, they know to call the planning specialist who handles their situation.

Since institutionalizing our service delivery, we are providing substantially better service than we were before. Our clients are much happier because their needs are being met on time. Now, we don't have to compete—we set the standards.

GRINDING

The grinding part is basically everything that supports the finding and minding functions. These activities are the backbone of your business. They include the less spectacular but critical functions of data management—paperwork processing, reporting, and financial plan manufacturing. Each activity needs to be broken down, analyzed, and then rebuilt to streamline your organization. These activities can be most easily systematized to enhance customer service and client perception of the value of your organization, while using technology to increase significantly the number of clients each planner can work with effectively.

The greatest limiting factor is the time necessary to conduct face-to-face meetings. Remember—affluent clients demand a personal relationship with their advisor. In addition to the in-person meetings, a planner must talk with clients on the phone, review update plans, make sure each plan is being implemented according to schedule, etc. Most practice management consultants agree that a planner providing some semblance of comprehensive planning would be hard pressed to work with 75 clients under the most efficient models. If you have larger clients with $3 to $5 million or more in assets, a planner would be very hard pressed to provide comprehensive advice, planning, and management to 25 clients.

Many practice management gurus suggest *firing* all but your 25 largest clients, but we believe this recommendation addresses only the symptoms, not the underlying problem. Many of the smaller clients with whom you would have to stop doing business are the same people who helped you get started in the first place. They continue to need your advice and counsel. We recognize that we owe much of our success to these clients. Also, larger clients require more of the organization's resources than smaller clients—at a ratio of 1 to 20. In addition, one of the first lessons learned in business school is never build a business model that is dependent on just a few clients.

The solution is to develop an integrated back-office service system, streamlining the grinding functions, to provide an infrastructure of uniform support. You may enable a planner to work very effectively with 100 clients of high net worth, and that's really a lot. If each of those 100 clients has $500,000 to invest on average, that's $50 million in assets under management. If each client you work with has $1 million in investment assets (which is more like our client base), that's $100 million in assets under management. So, if each planner in your office can work effectively with a client base having $100 million in aggregate assets under management and provide unparalleled services, nothing can stop your firm.

The only sure way to do that is to have a back-office service system that supports everything your planners do. The more you can rely on technology to handle certain functions, the less reliant you will be on the human factor.

Earlier, I mentioned a couple of software modules (trust management, minimum distribution requirements) that my firm uses to enhance client services. We have really developed several technology backbones:

- A sales-tracking program enables us to track all sales activities that relate to converting prospects into clients, from the initial contact with the prospect through payment of fees and commissions generated to the company and salespeople. Included is a complete tracking module ensuring timely investment transfers due to account changes.
- A client communication, event, and task-tracking program allows us to record all client communication and the resulting activities or tasks that the client contact generates. In addition, the event-tracking module lets us initiate and track to completion all client service items, whether one time or recurring.
- A service module program allows operations and administrative employees to flawlessly accomplish complex tasks. Examples previously given include trust management and minimum distribution service modules.
- A compliance program includes required records compliance for the NASD and SEC as well as making sure the company and salespeople are fully registered prior to initiating sales with clients.

The development of any technology solution is based on standard operating procedures. If no written procedures are in place, no checklist on how to accomplish a job from point A to point B, you have problems. We developed standard operating procedure manuals that cover step-by-step procedures for each process. In a lot of cases, there are checklists. You may find, like us, that the employees who actually do the work are the only logical choice to develop written procedures.

Because these folks are likely not expert in the process, *you must first develop a standard operating procedure for developing standard operating procedures* (SOPs). This step may sound ridiculous at first, but determining what a complete procedure looks like when it is finished is crucial to training your employees how to write the procedure.

When one of our employees develops a standard operating procedure, they start with our SOP development form. They write down what the procedure or task is in descriptive detail—in many cases, a checklist and a review by the employee's supervisor are conducted. When complete, we have another employee come in and attempt to perform the task, without help. We know the SOP works if the person gets it right the first time. Instead of written manuals, many SOPs have been imbedded into our service modules, further streamlining procedures and enhancing efficiency.

Each SOP should include the following:

- A written overview of the operation
- Specific instructions for the successful completion of the activity
- An explanation of how to use necessary software or files
- Sample checklist for each activity described
- An example of a properly completed document, report, or application (if applicable)

We actually promote redundant employee training based on our SOPs. Employees spend two hours per month doing each other's jobs so that everyone can learn the various tasks. Knowing from experience that people get sick or sometimes leave, maintain-

Sample SOP Development Checklist

Enter Title of Checklist

DATE: _____ BY: _____

Description of this operation:

Enter description, including purpose and desired outcome of the process outlined in this checklist.

Line Task Subtasks

1 Heading: describe outcome of the task set that follows here.

2 Describe task here.

3 List steps required to complete task.

4 List substeps.

5 Enter clarification to task or substeps.

6

7 Leave room for notes or data entry areas as needed.

8

9

10

11

12

13 Refer to line numbers if steps are to be skipped or repeated (example: Resume at line 15).

14

15

16

A footnote at the bottom of each page indicating when the procedure was developed or last modified.

ing operations can be a big problem. Like every other aspect of this business, your SOPs and checklists have to be continually updated.

Each and every task, though seemingly minor, is crucial to the success of the planner-client relationship. Developing the technology platform we have currently has taken us years and hundreds of thousands of dollars, and it is far from complete. You may not have the desire, knowledge, or capital to develop this type of technology to supercharge your practice. As you develop your strategic business plan, you may feel overwhelmed by all that needs to be accomplished. At this point, analyzing and pushing your resource partners, like your broker-dealer or custodian, to provide you with systems becomes crucial. These systems allow you to stay competitive, providing your clients with outstanding service.

21

Money Management

The qualities needed for successful money management are the same as those for creating a successful practice: standardization, uniformity, and developing standard operating procedures (SOPs). You can go really only one of two ways: adopt a turnkey asset management program or develop in-house money management systems yourself. Whether you go outside your firm to access third-party programs or develop your own money management products, you need to address what your competition is offering, the direction of product development in the industry, and the specific needs of your target market.

We have observed over the years that clients move through an identifiable *lifecycle of investing*. During the early years, as they begin to earn and save money, they are in the *accumulation stage* of their investment lifecycle. This stage is characterized by the fact that the amount they are saving is much more important to their success as an investor than the return they achieve on their modest account balance. For example, the success of a 30-year-old who has a $10,000 investment account and who is adding $500 per month is much more dependent on the continued savings ($6,000/year) than on the account's investment return of 10 percent ($1,000/year).

Life Cycle of Investing

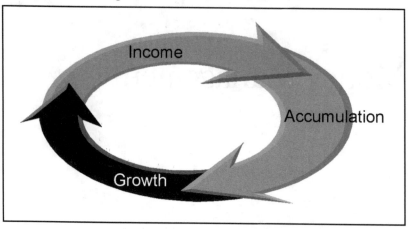

Even if the investment return on the account increased dramatically to 12 percent, the additional growth is not nearly as important as continuing the systematic savings plan. It is our experience that investors in the accumulation phase are usually aggressive, looking to capture high rates of return even though they must take high risk to do so. Many have stated that, at this stage of their life, they believe if they lose their money, they can easily replace it through savings in a relatively short time.

Most investors begin to change their perceptions about risk as they accumulate more assets through savings and investment and their account balance becomes significant, requiring years to replace if lost. Clients at this stage move into the *growth stage* of their investment lifecycle. By revisiting the same client 15 years later at age 45, we see that the client's account balance has grown substantially to $252,000 (assuming the same savings pattern and a 10 percent rate of return). As clients move further out along this growth phase toward retirement, they eventually reach a point where they could never replace lost assets because they simply do not have enough time left. Clients are well aware of this fact and tend to become more conservative. At this stage, clients typically tell us they would like returns that are high enough to achieve their objectives while assuming significantly less risk to their principal. Because their asset base has grown significantly, the return they achieve on their account becomes much more important than their additional savings.

As clients stop working and begin to withdraw income from their account, their investment objectives and risk profile change again. This is the *income stage* of their investment lifecycle where they focus on income to support their lifestyle needs, and their investment focus shifts to reducing principal risk. Achieving return becomes a secondary objective. Clients at this point in their investment life have spent their lives accumulating and growing their investment account and cannot afford to lose it. They often tell us that this is all the money they have: "It is our serious money that we cannot afford to lose."

These broad investment themes regarding what clients want at different stages of their investment lifecycle need to be integrated into your product offerings. When we take on a financial planning client, establishing a fiduciary relationship and developing a plan to help them accomplish their objectives, we take on a much higher degree of responsibility than others in the investment industry. Other investment professionals develop investment products that may or may not work effectively; we develop investment solutions for clients that must work if our clients are to meet their goals.

As part of our strategic business plan, we analyzed our target clients' investment needs, products offered by our competition, and trends in product development to determine the best design for our fee-based money management products. This analysis led us to identify several strategic objectives for our products. The following list may help you determine what investment products you need to offer:

- Our money management products must add value to clients over and above the cost of our fees. The value we add must be measurable by normally accepted portfolio statistical standards.
- Our product design must provide clients with the rate of return and risk experience they need to achieve their goals as determined through the financial planning process.

- Our products should be designed as a total investment solution, allowing us to capture all the client's assets.
- Our products should be different. We don't want to fight for product shelf space on the same shelf as other money managers. We would like to create a new shelf.
- Our products need to be institutional quality to be competitive and allow for broad distribution.

When designing or sourcing your money management offerings for clients, keep in mind that a manager can only accomplish one of three objectives: They can manage risk, providing safety of principal; manage for capital appreciation (highest return); or manage for tax efficiency. Most products offered today are managed to produce highest return without regard for safety of principal or tax efficiency. We see this changing with new product offerings focusing on risk management and tax efficiency. Beware of product offerings that proclaim to meet all three objectives at the same time. From our own experience, we know that you can really only try to target one investment objective as your primary goal. If your goal is highest return, you really can't worry about safety of principal and may need to generate short-term gains to capture return.

We identified our target market as the senior market in or very near retirement. They have accumulated considerable assets and their number one priority is not to lose them. They want a high enough return to outpace inflation and taxes while maintaining a conservative to moderate risk profile. Armed with a detailed understanding of our target client, we developed what we believe are unique money management products designed to provide these clients with exactly what they want: risk-managed growth and risk-managed income. These investors have told us that their number one priority is not to lose the money they worked so hard to accumulate; second, they want a rate of return high enough to outpace inflation and taxes; and third, they want to keep taxes to a minimum.

Our products focus on providing investors with low relative risk, a rate of return high enough to meet their objectives, and, because taxes affect returns dramatically, as much tax efficiency as possible while ensuring safety of principal. After identifying your target clients's investment priorities, you need to look at the competitive forces in the marketplace and determine how they are driving client perceptions.

Ten years ago, investment advisors could provide clients with consolidated quarterly reports and passive strategic asset allocation using mutual funds, rebalancing once per year. Folks started out paying fairly high fees for investment management services that were not terribly difficult to perform, but competitive pressures have changed clients' perceptions dramatically.

On the self-developed side, you have to make sure that the money management service or product you're offering is competitive in today's environment. One of the biggest problems with the current state of affairs for asset allocators is that the competitive marketplace is moving against them. For instance, Vanguard provides strategic asset allocation and rebalancing for clients at no cost. So, if you're a fee-based money manager using passive asset allocation and rebalancing, your product offering isn't going to work over the long haul because mutual funds and annuities are already providing these services for free.

We can't stress this often enough: *Look at what the client actually wants.* In the beginning of the 1990s, people wanted a consolidated report on their investment positions, and that was something they were willing to pay for. The next step was to provide asset allocation based on Modern Portfolio Theory with passive reallocation once a year, but passive reallocation has moved a quarterly schedule. Folks started out paying fairly high fees for a task that wasn't terribly difficult to perform and didn't require a lot of activity. Advisors basically invested the client's money, then reviewed their portfolio quarterly to see if the funds selected were performing up to snuff and rebalancing the portfolio to bring it back into compliance with the allocation. Clients today don't assign a significant value to this process because they can get those services free of charge. Purveyors of these services are being priced right out of the market.

If you're going to be in the asset management business, what do you have to offer? Certainly you must have investment management reporting. It's no longer a commodity that has any value, though, because clients can get it at no charge from Quicken. Quicken software will interface with Schwab, for example, so you can download all your investment positions daily. From a client's perspective, how important is quarterly reporting on their investments? Not very.

One of the things clients want in this age of instant gratification is to see you, as their investment manager, respond to the environment. In other words, they want to see change. They want to know that you are not asleep at the switch, that you are effectively providing some type of oversight and value to their portfolio management for the fee you're charging. Clients experiencing normal volatility in the markets perceive that their manager's job is to make changes in portfolio allocation as market and economic conditions change. If not, they quickly become disenchanted with paying fees for a service that they perceive as not active enough.

We think that strategic passive asset allocation may not be attractive to clients anymore, because they want to see that you are reviewing the portfolio and responding to the dynamic investment environment.

I find it especially interesting that the Securities and Exchange Commission (SEC) requires an account to be under continuous supervision. In order to meet the SEC's registration requirements, you must actively manage an account. If you're doing passive strategic asset allocation and annual rebalancing and charging a fee for it, you don't qualify. It doesn't matter if you have $100 million, $200 million, or $500 million under management: If you're not actively managing those accounts, then according to the SEC, you're not providing continuous supervision. The whole game on the investment side is changing dramatically. If you're doing in-house investment management, you need to look at what you're offering and up your game significantly to respond to 1) what clients want and 2) what you can actually charge fees for.

From a money management standpoint, you must reassess what you offer clients and make sure it's going to be competitive over the next five years as the industry changes. For example, our money management process adds significant value. We have discretionary authority over client accounts, which are under constant supervision. We have designed our portfolio management process to incorporate strategic allocation for a portion of the portfolio and tactical sector allocation for the balance of the portfolio.

We also integrate proprietary risk management methodology to reduce risk, providing clients with an investment experience that makes them comfortable. A lot of active management is being provided. We do that because our whole focus is to provide high rates of return to meet the client's objectives while providing a low-risk, low-volatility investment experience at the same time. We bring different things together in the portfolio design process to get the job done. Our clients know that we're not asleep at the switch—they know we're working all the time because they see changes in the portfolio.

We've educated them on our whole investment management process. They know it's completely different from others, and even though we have a very successful money management process, we still need to respond to what the customer or client wants.

One change taking place in our industry today is the tremendous marketing push being made by wrap fee program providers. It seems that virtually everyone in the financial service industry is extolling the benefits of separate account management using individual securities. Wrap advocates argue that a program customized by using world-class individual securities managers better serves clients. They add that because these customized accounts are not grouped with other investors, they can easily exclude securities or industries their clients don't want and can be managed to provide tax efficiency that mutual funds can't duplicate. A pretty compelling argument and one that we hear parroted by some of our existing clients and most new prospects.

Due to the bull market of the 1990s, many of our existing clients, and most new clients, have investment portfolios that have grown beyond the need to have all of their assets invested in only our risk-managed portfolios. They have sufficient "serious money" assets already allocated to accomplish their fundamental objectives, allowing a portion to be invested for capital appreciation or tax efficiency without regard to risk. Also, as we upgrade our target market to include clients with a larger asset base, we need to provide the right investment solutions to accomplish their objectives—and that sometimes means allocating investment assets away from our in-house program to other managers.

To this end, we've built a wrap fee product, utilizing Schwab's MAC Program, that integrates our core money management philosophy and our in-house products. Clients invest enough of their assets to ensure their goals are met in our risk-managed programs, and the balance is allocated to style-specific individual security managers who complement our security holdings. Our clients are excited by the benefits of integrating two completely different programs. They like the peace of mind our risk-managed program provides for their serious money, and they like the greater return opportunity and tax efficiency that the wrap product provides for the balance of their assets.

You must respond to what's needed. If everybody else has separate account managers, wrap fee programs, then you'd better offer them, too, or you're going to lose some client assets. We can't add the kind of separate account management a wrap product provides in-house, where you have a value stock picker and a small-company growth guy and a big-cap value guy, etc. I don't know any other financial planning operation in the country that can integrate all of the portfolio managers, analysts, staff, and technology required to replicate that kind of thing. Really, you have to go outside to find folks to provide these products to your clients.

We're in the process of evaluating our resource partners to determine whether they're the right ones for us to get the job done. When you're affiliated with a broker-dealer or other entity, you must make sure they can provide the services your client needs and that they are prepared to adapt to the client's changing needs.

Our typical affluent client used to have $500,000. Now, most of those people have $1 million or more, and many of our clients have from $2 million to $5 million to invest. They're starting to approach superaffluent stages, and there are a lot more of those people. It's been predicted that the number of people with $1 million in investable assets will increase at a rate of 17 percent per year over the next ten years. We've got to find a way to work with these clients and provide them with the services that the big firms will provide. Banks, insurance companies, and brokerage firms are all going to offer completely integrated family-office services, including financial planning, accounting advice, legal advice, investment management, banking, mortgage origination, trust services, etc. You're going to have to decide how you're going to offer these services. How do you provide turnkey family-office management services when they integrate across all these disciplines? The solution is partnering with the right company or companies.

I have a client whose home mortgage is held by Merrill Lynch. He was given a 30-year, 100 percent financing, interest-only mortgage. Merrill allows highly compensated execs and business owners to borrow money at a more favorable rate than they can get anyplace else, but they're told, "In order to keep your loan at the lowest rate, we have to have all your money." My client has $300,000 of his account collateralizing this loan. In this example, for us to move the client so that we can bring the money under management, we have to be able to replace the loan on terms at least as favorable as Merrill's. That's tough to do, and it's just one example of the kind of services you'll have to offer to compete in today's market.

Mark Hurley, president of Undiscovered Funds in Dallas, has predicted that in the near future, maybe 20 brand-name megacompanies will be providing wealth management services. My concern for all of us—my firm included—is that if you cannot become a brand name and harness technology, you will have trouble surviving the coming competitive onslaught. None of us want to go from "I had a great financial planning business and was making a lot of money." to "I have never worked so hard in my life for so little money."

Competition is heating up, and anybody who doesn't see that is kidding herself. So, you have a choice. You can be competitive and offer the highest value, cutting-edge service while building an institutional-quality company—not just a sales practice, not a job that you can't sell, but a business that's worth something. Or, you can ignore all of the warnings about change in the industry and large competitors taking your clients. Maybe your sales practice (high paying job) will provide you with just as much income in the future as it has in the past.

Make the choice not just to survive but to *thrive*, by building an organization that has a relationship with the client—a dependent relationship where the client relies on the *organization* for all of the services they need and wouldn't think of going someplace else. Then your client retention will be high and the value of your business will rise accordingly. You will not only be competitive, you can set the standard for competition. Standards that, hopefully, others will find difficult to meet.

PART 5

The End Game

22

Financial Advisory Business of the Future

In the future, a virtual advisory *team* will most effectively provide global advice for the affluent on a completely integrated basis providing advice, service, and management across all areas of a client's financial life. This virtual advisory team will integrate accounting, legal, insurance, banking, and investment functions—everything financial a client needs, much like a family office provides for clients with extreme wealth.

The latest technology will enable the financial planning family office of the future to completely integrate the financial experience of the client and have only one point of contact, one portal through which all advice and service flow, the planner. Large private banks and private trust companies have long offered a family office service to wealthy clients with $100 million or more in assets. It's a turnkey environment encompassing legal services, accounting, bookkeeping, bill paying, estate planning, and investment management. You name it—they do it. They walk the dog and negotiate employment contracts. They provide business management services and business planning advice. They integrate a complete, very high-touch financial solution for wealthy families.

Some of the most wealthy families in the country, like the Rockefellers, have built their own family offices that employ hundreds of people to manage their wealth and provide services to family members. Bessemer Trust Company is one family office company, started to manage one family's fortune. Over a period of years, the company has changed their strategy to include about 300 wealthy families. Companies like Bessemer are broadening their competitive stance and moving downmarket in terms of client size, creating even more competition for clients in the superaffluent $10 to $50 million client target market.

We can use technology to systematize the delivery of turnkey financial advice and management to the point where we no longer need hundreds of millions of dollars to replicate this level of service for wealthy people. We can offer it to the merely affluent client with $1 million or several million dollars of assets to manage and provide them with the same level of advice and service formerly reserved only for the superwealthy.

UTILIZING MULTISERVICE CHANNELS

Your business model has to be robust enough to capture clients, controlling their access points to financial advice and management. Clients must be able to communicate with you and access their account information at several different service points—face-to-face, by telephone, with your knowledgeable support staff independent of you, by e-mail, and through complete Web-based service offerings.

The face-to-face channel is the traditional way of utilizing financial services. Many clients still prefer that channel. They want to be able to access you and deal with you on a face-to-face basis. Older clients in the senior category want a trusted advisor to deal with directly and will never be comfortable dealing through a technology medium. But other clients will be just as happy never seeing a financial planner. If you can provide advice and service over the Internet at a quality level that's acceptable to them, they will never come and see you. And that means that you can do financial planning for anybody, anywhere in the world. Clients don't need to call or see you to find out how much their account has gone up or down that day. They just go online and get their performance reporting and a complete status list of all open service items requiring their attention. You can deliver significant advice and service directly to clients over the Web at a lower price point than what you can offer through traditional service models. Being all things to all people is difficult, but we think technology allows us to level the playing field with the largest competitors in the industry.

Currently, a tremendous interest is building in acquiring financial planning or investment advisory service companies, and a deluge of money is available to grow businesses. Many of the largest players in our industry are acquiring service professionals across the complete spectrum of financial advice and service. American Express has adopted an acquisition strategy to integrate financial planning, accounting, legal advice, banking, investment, and insurance by buying professionals and companies in each space. While large capitalized players can pursue acquisitions, most planners do not have the capital or scale to adopt this strategy. Smaller firms have to develop strategies to compete effectively, and for most of us, strategic joint ventures with other professionals offer the greatest opportunity.

Joint ventures allow two or more parties with a common focus and goals to come together and develop a uniform strategy, enabling them to become more competitive. Many other professionals are looking to enter our industry as an opportunity to profit from the growth in affluence in our country. For many years, regulation has prevented them from accepting compensation for advice or service in any form other than hourly fees. But the regulatory environment is undergoing a radical shift to allow allied professionals to accept any form of compensation and to provide a wide variety of advice and service outside their core business. Financial planners have an unparalleled opportunity to be catalysts for change by becoming a channel for allied professionals to enter the industry, helping them develop or use their institutional financial planning business models as a portal to transact business.

If you're the quarterback, the portal through which the client gets all advice and service, how can you use this to your advantage? By utilizing technology, especially the World Wide Web, to tie your joint venture partners together into a virtual advisory service team. Together you will provide clients with a level of advice and service that competitors cannot duplicate. Nothing like this virtual model exists in our industry today; we need to build it.

In the old way of doing business, I would use multiple channels in terms of marketing and making referrals to CPAs and lawyers. Today, the opportunity lies in creating a multichannel joint venture virtual community. Instead of having a loose referral affiliation, we are building a virtual advisory team, tying all these people in to become an engine of turnkey financial advice and management.

As financial planners, we act as the financial quarterback for the client and as the portal through which our professional joint

Global Planning for Affluent Clients

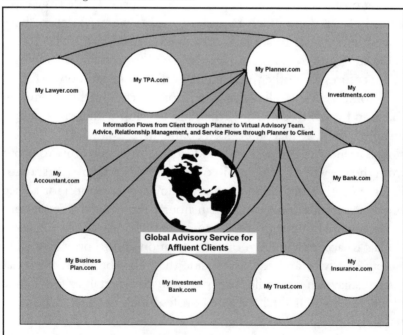

venture partners interact. All parties interconnect through a common technology platform, communicating seamlessly and collaborating on the clients' behalf. Our combined referral sources increase the level of business across the entire group, and we think the revenue opportunity is unparalleled.

For instance, you need lawyers to do documentation, but you don't want to refer clients to outside professionals because sooner than later, accountants and lawyers will offer financial planning advice and investment services. So you go to the law firm and say: *We're a multichannel marketing group. I propose that you refer all your clients to us for financial planning, and we'll refer all of our clients to you for estate planning.* You need to create a formal joint venture with these partners and document your working agreement. Everybody knows what they are responsible for and what they get out of the relationship, and everybody makes more money that way. Eventually, all revenue will be shared across joint venture parties.

STRATEGIC VENTURES

CPAs, attorneys, third-party administrators (TPAs), and trust companies are all looking to get into the financial planning business. Many small-sized to medium-sized firms do not have the resource base required to build a financial planning, money management program from scratch. They're looking for resource partners to leverage themselves into the business. They also don't want to lose their core business to another full-service entity. To compete effectively, you must provide affluent clients with the turnkey platform they want.

Create strategic joint ventures where you get the services that they can provide and you're not replicating that service cost in your business plan. Make sure you're gaining something for it—like access to their client base. This is a win-win situation.

A joint venture means a *formal* agreement and possibly a separate entity co-owned by each partner. In the case of a financial planner and a CPA firm, you would probably create a separate joint venture company, most likely registered as an investment advisor in the states where you have clients. *Stock* could be shared on an equal or some other basis, but with formalized contracts.

In most states, lawyers are further behind CPAs in terms of accepting compensation other than hourly or retainer legal fees. I suggest that you use attorneys for what they're doing now—tie into their resource base on the referral side. Instead of a loose affiliation where you refer some clients for estate planning, create a joint venture agreement whereby your company offers estate planning services through your joint venture partner. Establish a trial relationship and expand that relationship as the environment, regulatory and otherwise, changes. Multidisciplinary practices (MDPs) are getting a lot of press, and members of the accounting and legal profession are applying significant pressure to be allowed to create MDPs.

Become an expert. Be a leader in creating these types of practices. Show your partners how to create synergy, making the most of joint ventures. You can create a very large virtual organization quickly with very little expense. Each one of these joint ventures will probably cost you less than $50,000 in terms of legal fees and consulting.

RESOURCE PARTNERS

As you build your business plan, you may wonder, *How am I going to get everything done?* You can do it all yourself, but I believe that one of the keys to your successful business plan will be to determine what you need from *resource partners* such as your broker-dealer, trust company, or an investment banking company for your business owner clients.

Take your business plan to your broker-dealer and ask what they can do to help you implement it. Make sure they completely understand your business plan, then let them show you how they can apply their larger resource base to help you be competitive.

Most independent broker-dealers are looking for ways to add value to their relationships with their representatives, and may have started to look into facilitating some type of business planning for their significant producers. For some broker-dealers, this may be a new idea, but eventually all will come to recognize that they must find a way to help their field force compete more effectively for affluent and wealthy clients.

The independents need to be careful how they implement their own strategy. According to our view of the future, the $350,000 broker on which they're focusing their current recruiting efforts is not likely to be competitive in the near future. Most are not building sustainable financial planning businesses, so they will fail to provide consumers with the services they want. Many will go out of business. Brokerage firms would be far better served to concentrate their resources on building existing financial planning franchises.

Few, if any, of the top 20 broker-dealers do strategic business planning for themselves, much less for reps. The bigger the organization, the harder to start and integrate strategic planning. The closest thing we have to a significant resource partner is broker-

Resource Partners

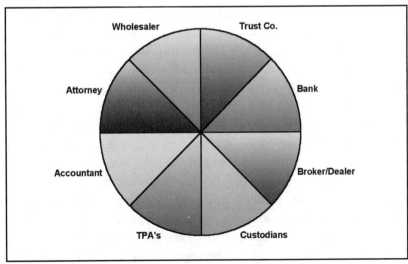

dealers, who are desperately trying to find a way to add value to the relationship. They don't want us just to end up doing business with Schwab or somebody else, where we can get a higher payout or a signing bonus.

Broker-dealers are all trying to find a way to lock in big offices, and they're missing what's right under their noses. If they help to facilitate strategic business planning for their reps, expending some resources on providing these services, then they're going to have more business than they can handle. Wholesalers from product manufacturers can also be an excellent resource to help facilitate planning. My belief is that they should channel their marketing dollars to these types of programs instead of wasting so much money buying reps dinner or entertaining them at conferences. I don't know about you, but I can afford to buy myself dinner or travel on vacation. What I really need is a collaborative focus from these partners to help us increase our business and accomplish our business objectives. This is truly a win-win, not only for us but also for the broker-dealers and product manufacturers. As we increase the size of our business, we will increase the amount of business we do through them.

One of the great developments today is that 130 universities have undergraduate degree programs in family financial management or financial planning and teach the Certified Financial Planner (CFP) curriculum—and the number's growing by probably 50 percent a year. Young people are coming out of these universities with a knowledge base that is incredible. For a fraction of what a company would risk on someone who's untrained, it can hire graduates of financial planning programs. Five years ago, only a handful of such graduates were available; now hundreds graduate every year. We recruit these college students from all over the country for entry-level service and sales positions.

Remember when the practice management gurus were telling everybody to downsize their business? They were focusing on the problem and not the solution. They were advising you to throw away clients who were the best marketing partners you could ever have. I'm advising that you do the opposite. If you can't *personally* handle any more business, let's change the way you run your business and bring in the resources (new salespeople) to mine the hundreds of referrals that your existing clients can provide you. With hundreds more referrals from new clients, you can build an institutional business very quickly. Align your resource partners' interest with your business objectives, share your business plan with them, and get them to help implement your plan by tapping into their larger resource base. It will be good business for you and them.

23

Valuation

If your objective is to build a business with significant equity value, first you must understand what determines value.

A financial planning or investment advisory practice would be considered a professional practice for valuation purposes. While a professional practice has characteristics similar to most other small businesses, it also has some characteristics that make it unique:

- A professional practice is a service business with few tangible assets.
- The professional develops a trusted relationship with clients.
- New clients are usually generated from referrals from existing clients.
- Professionals have to meet regulatory, licensing, and education requirements.
- Most of the value of the practice is tied to the professional and the goodwill they create.

The three primary methods used by valuation experts today are:

1. *Income method.* Expected or projected future cash flow is discounted to present value at an appropriate rate of return for the investment an acquirer will make in the company.
2. *Market value method.* This method compares other market-based transactions involving companies that are similar to financial planning/investment advisory businesses, then adjusts for size and other material factors that are dissimilar.
3. *Asset-based method.* This method restates the assets and liabilities of the business from historical cost (book value) to fair market value.

However, these valuation methods fail to adequately address *continuity* issues, causing some valuation experts to arrive at too conservative a value to ever effect a transaction. To properly value a financial services practice, the focus should be on the ability of the business to generate *predictable* cash flow and, therefore, profit. Predictable cash flow is dependent on recurring revenue streams and the level of client, employee, and revenue retention.

RECURRING REVENUE

Over the past ten years, almost everyone in the financial services industry has learned that recurring revenue streams are more valuable than nonrecurring, commission-based income.

Recurring revenue can take many forms; for example, advisory fees, planning fees, update planning fees, insurance renewals, mutual fund trails, group insurance, and group retirement plan fees/commissions. When determining the value of your company, a potential acquirer or partner is likely to evaluate each of these income streams differently, because the likelihood of retaining the revenue depends on its type.

The value of a revenue stream also depends on the acquirer's business model—whether the revenue stream is part of its core business strategy. For example, a bank or mutual fund organization might place little, if any, value on insurance renewal income streams, when their business model focuses on assets under fee-based investment management. For most planners, the greatest recurring revenue gain will come from converting to fee-based investment programs any and all client investment assets not already positioned in them.

CLIENT RETENTION

Any potential acquirer or partner will look at your historical financials to determine value. They will look at key financial performance components of revenue, expense, and profit as well as growth trends over the past five years. Unfortunately, historical performance only gives them a realistic picture of the organization with the current owners/principals in place and provides little, if any, evidence of how much client and employee attrition is likely to occur post-acquisition. The ultimate question any acquirer must answer is how much of the current revenue streams will they keep after a transition takes place.

For your organization to have significant value, your clients must be comfortable that they will continue to receive the same level of advice and service from your organization under any and all circumstances. To accomplish this, you must transfer the relationship that the client has developed with the owner/principal or planner to the organization or, as we have discussed, *institutionalize the client relationship*. Based on our experience, this process takes about two to three years, but when service and advice responsibility is shifted to the organization, the client is more likely to stay if the principals leave, retire, merge, or sell the organization. Over time, your clients become aware that a lot of the advice and service they value is being delivered not by you, but by your organization and your employees. This institutional relationship with clients is a key factor in determining the ultimate value of the organization to a potential acquirer.

EMPLOYEE RETENTION

In a financial services business, you cannot provide clients with advice, service, and relationship management without your employees. Therefore, ensuring employee retention is key to building value in your organization. As your company grows, you will also need to compete effectively for top talent.

To attract and tie key employees to your company, they will need to be able to achieve their own personal financial and career aspirations within your company. They will be looking to you as *the owner* to show them that achieving their visions will be possible. Your long hours and diligence in developing your strategic business plan pays great dividends right here. With your strategic business plan, you now have an ethical tool, possibly for the first time, to show employees how the business will develop over the next five to ten years and the career opportunities that will be available to them.

You must include long-term incentive plans focusing on profit and equity sharing. Many owners have philosophical problems with sharing a "piece of the rock" and often wait until they have lost key people before implementing these plans.

THE DFCF VALUATION APPROACH

Because service organizations are often difficult to value—much of the value is derived from intangibles such as goodwill and employee knowledge—we have determined the best valuation method for a financial services practice is a discounted future cash flow (DFCF) approach, with some new twists added to take into account specific retention issues. This type of valuation has two advantages over other traditional methods: It focuses on the key drivers of goodwill, and it establishes a reasonable empirical method of arriving at fair value for buyer and seller.

The drivers of goodwill are:

- Expected future revenue
- Historical revenues, expenses, profits, and cash flow
- Quality of balance sheet
- Types of revenue streams
- Fee schedule
- Attrition rates
- Level of competition in area
- Quality of referral base
- Demographics of client base
- Quality of employee base
- Employment agreements, non-compete agreements, and confidentiality agreements
- Practice location
- Reputation of practice

To incorporate and assess these goodwill factors, a valuation model must quantify the following:

- What services are being provided?
- Are they the comprehensive services that affluent clients desire?
- How well are these services being delivered?
- How does the organization leverage the use of technology in delivering client services? Marketing?
- What are the demographics of the client base?
- What is the history of client and revenue attrition over the past three years?
- Is client attrition high or low and why?
- How are new clients gathered?
- How strong are referral sources?
- How much and what percentage of revenue do the five largest clients contribute?
- What percentage of the clients are fee based?
- What are the total recurring revenue sources?
- How much revenue is generated by each source?
- How likely is the acquirer to retain this revenue?

- Who are the key employees? Will they stay?
- What services do they provide?
- What is their compensation?
- Are there standard operating procedures in writing that define all critical functions and tasks performed in the business?
- Has the relationship with the client been institutionalized?

Let's look at an example of the valuation effects of recurring revenue and institutionalizing client relationships on a financial planning practice. Illustrated below is the 1997 year-end revenue and expense figures used to determine the value of Anne's commission-based sales practice in January 1998.

EXAMPLE Anne's Commission-Based Practice Valuation

Business Profile	Commission-Based Sales Practice
Existing Assets Invested in Load Funds	$60,000,000
New Money Invested in Load Product	$10,000,000
Existing Assets Under Fee Management	$ 0
New Assets Under Management	$ 0
Overhead Expense Factor (% of Gross Income)	46.00%
Retention Assumptions	
Financial Planning Fees	25.00%
Equity Commissions	12.50%
Equity Trails	25.00%
Asset Management Fees	50.00%
Group Compensation	50.00%
Insurance Commissions	0.00%
Value	$311,077

We can see from the valuation, Anne will not be well rewarded for having built a pretty substantial commission-based sales practice.

As she began to develop her business plan in the spring of 1998, Anne recognized right away that she could increase the value of her practice by converting commission-based mutual fund assets to fee-based investment programs. She is immediately successful in converting one-quarter of client assets to fees, and the effect on her business value is quite dramatic.

Anne's Practice Value with a Little Planning and Recurring Revenue

Business Profile	Commission-Based Sales Practice	Fee-Based Sales Practice
Existing Assets Invested in Load Funds	$60,000,000	$41,250,000
New Money Invested in Load Product	$10,000,000	$10,000,000
Existing Assets Under Fee Management	$ 0	$15,000,000
New Assets Under Management	$ 0	$13,750,000
Overhead Expense Factor (% of Gross Income)	46.00%	55.00%
Retention Assumptions		
Financial Planning Fees	25.00%	25.00%
Equity Commissions	12.50%	12.50%
Equity Trails	25.00%	25.00%
Asset Management Fees	50.00%	50.00%
Group Compensation	50.00%	50.00%
Insurance Commissions	0.00%	0.00%
Value	$311,077	$616,920

The addition of recurring fee-based investment revenue through the conversion of commission-based mutual funds and focusing future asset gathering toward fee-based investment programs will double the value of Anne's business—even with the higher expense factor due to hiring more staff.

But the big boost in equity value comes from institutionalizing the client relationship and service delivery. The acquirer would be compelled to increase the revenue retention assumptions because they are confident that the organization will provide continuity of cash flow by achieving high levels of client retention.

The value of Anne's fee-based business is *five times* the value of her commission-based sales practice. The combination of increasing recurring revenue streams and institutionalizing her relationship with her clients, as well as upgrading the quality of her organization, will pay handsome dividends if she decides to sell her business to fund her retirement.

As more financial planning businesses change hands, the key value drivers of recurring revenue, enterprisewide advice, and service leading to highly predictable client retention will become much more mainstream in valuation models.

Not every planner will want to build an institutional quality business with a large infrastructure, but those who can may find a larger well-capitalized partner, a *strategic buyer,* who will provide them with an exit opportunity that may well astound them. Large financial companies across every segment of the financial, brokerage, banking, trust, and insurance industries are looking for a business model that is scalable and will allow them to provide financial planning to large numbers of affluent and wealthy consumers. Even smaller firms who upgrade their sales practice to an institutional quality business will be able to increase the value of their business dramatically while increasing the quality of life for everyone around them: clients, employees, and family.

Anne's Sales Practice Converted to an Institutional Quality Business

Business Profile	Commission-Based Sales Practice	Fee-Based Sales Practice	Fee-Based Business
Existing Assets Invested in Load Funds	$60,000,000	$41,250,000	$41,250,000
New Money Invested in Load Product	$10,000,000	$10,000,000	$10,000,000
Existing Assets Under Fee Management	$ 0	$15,000,000	$15,000,000
New Assets Under Management	$ 0	$13,750,000	$17,500,000
Overhead Expense Factor (% of Gross Income)	46.00%	55.00%	55.00%
Retention Assumptions			
Financial Planning Fees	25.00%	25.00%	85.00%
Equity Commissions	12.50%	12.50%	50.00%
Equity Trails	25.00%	25.00%	50.00%
Asset Management Fees	50.00%	50.00%	85.00%
Group Compensation	50.00%	50.00%	85.00%
Insurance Commissions	0.00%	0.00%	25.00%
Value	$311,077	$616,920	$1,465,071

24

Exit Strategies

As you're developing your strategic business plan, you should decide how you'd like to leave your business. Because of the problems associated with providing continuity for clients, shareholders, and employees, *succession planning* should be a top priority that is integrated into your strategic business plan.

SUCCESSION PLANNING

To develop a successful succession plan, you must build a sustainable, profitable business with equity stakeholder employees who will implement your plan even though you are not present day to day to manage them. You will not only need to train these employees, you must also give them time to mature as salespeople and planners, as well as managers and executives. Identify and groom someone to take over the key management and sales functions that you now provide.

Sales and management continuity are critical to retaining clients and revenue and thus, equity value. Your clients need time to get to know and trust new planners. During this transitional period, you need to continue to be the "trusted advisor" until your protégés establish their own relationships with your client base. This process usually takes a minimum of three to five years to implement.

Without proper planning, you may find yourself without much income or value due to client attrition and employee defection. A good succession plan seamlessly replaces departing sales and executive talent (owners) with new, highly motivated, well-trained employees. In retirement, the last thing you want to do is to wake up one morning to the nightmare of not having the income you were banking on, and having to start working twice as hard as you used to, to resurrect a faltering business and earn your buyout.

Always remember, as long as the business depends on you for success, beyond your strategic role as an owner, your business will not have significant value.

As an owner, you can employ a number of effective exit strategies to maximize shareholder value:

- Retain an equity and income interest and walk away from day-to-day responsibilities.
- Sell to another professional.
- Sell to your employees.
- Sell to a larger, unrelated third party such as a bank, trust company, or consolidator.

My current plan is to retain my interest, but that doesn't mean I won't change my mind. I will probably retain my interest until I am no longer willing to do what's required of an owner, to create a vision for where the business is going while establishing strategy and ensuring implementation of the plan.

When a business owner is no longer willing to provide these functions, they should walk away or sell the business. You probably cannot find someone to do all the things an owner does but who doesn't want to own your interest. Ordinarily, anyone who has the knowledge and talent to run your business will either already own a business or will want your owner's interest to stay motivated.

Retire Retaining an Income Interest and Your Equity

The way I built my practice was by cold-calling on business owners in New Jersey. I would walk into the businesses' headquarters and ask for the owners by name. Very often, as much as 30 or 40 percent of the time, I would be told that the owner only visited the company once or twice a year. In fact, the owners often lived outside the country, but they continued to earn a significant income stream from their ownership interest. They had not only created an institutional quality business, but they had successfully replaced themselves in their business.

If you build your business correctly to the point where someone else can run it, you can retain a board position or act as a key officer of the organization. This role will allow you to maintain a significant, ongoing income. You may arrange a consulting contract with the company, or you may prefer to retain some ongoing duties as an employee. Certain equity recapitalization techniques would also allow you to earn a significant cash flow on the equity position you retain in your company.

I have a friend who has a well-established planning practice. He's in his mid-60s and is looking to transition out of his daily sales and management role, but he wants to retain an equity and income interest. He will continue to guide the company in implementing his strategic plan. He also wants to be the "ambassador of goodwill" and will continue to manage his existing client relationships.

The company holds several client appreciation seminars or dinners per year, which allow him to continue to meet with all the clients of his firm. He also wants to continue to see several clients who have become close friends. He meets with these folks several times a quarter and is also called on to handle the handful of clients who still prefer to deal with him directly. He has transferred the rest of his client base to other planners and key employees that he's trained over the past three years. Not only have his employees retained what he built, but they've also continued to increase the size of the business.

Employees are compensated predominantly from the growth of the business. His personal income has stayed level or increased slightly each year, because he made the tough decision years ago to reinvest in his business to build up staff, *institutionalizing* his organization.

We have been following that plan with my company for the past six or seven years. Instead of continuing to max out income (eat what we kill), we have reinvested in the business to build infrastructure and grow our firm. We believe the only way to grow is to reinvest cash flow and profit to create a world-class business with significant shareholder value. Over the years, we have reduced the sales compensation payouts in our company across the board. Following the industry model in place at the time, our key sales executives routinely, took 70 to 80 percent of each revenue dollar out of the company in sales compensation. Today our top sales compensation payout is 50 percent, reflecting the need to reinvest in the business. But, because of the advances we have made to our business model, our sales professionals can handle more clients with ease. By focusing on recurring revenue, technology enhanced workflow processes, and institutionalizing client relationships, our salespeople are making more than ever before. They tell us the greatest benefit that they have garnered is a higher quality personal life. They are not the cog in the wheel, trapped in our old sales practice service model.

Selling to Another Professional

Maybe you don't have the employees within your organization with the strength of character, knowledge, and commitment required to take over your business, or perhaps you're at a stage in your career where you don't have five or ten years to groom somebody. In that case, you might want to consider someone outside your company—perhaps a friend or a local competitor who you feel would be a good fit for your clients. You could approach this individual with an offer to enter into a buy-sell agreement, so that if you were to become disabled or to die prematurely, or if you wanted to retire, they would buy your business. Or you could decide to create a joint venture and become partners, or even merge your practices to provide continuity of management and succession planning for older owners. Many independent broker-dealers will not only help set up this type of arrangement but will finance the buyout.

Employee Buyouts

As financial planning and investment advisory companies grow in size and scale, an Employee Stock Ownership Plan (ESOP) might become an evolving succession strategy to consider. Although I think it's a little too early for most practices to do today, certainly some of the larger planning and investment management businesses could look to an ESOP to provide a solution for shareholder buyouts as an exit strategy for retiring owners. These businesses typically have achieved sufficient size to ensure future continuity for all shareholders and employees.

An ESOP can allow an organization to achieve greater scale while retaining its independence, instead of being forced to sell to a third party to fund the retirement of founding partners. The risk to an ESOP buyout is not usually to the departing shareholder(s) but to the employees who will fund the buyout, and it should be carefully analyzed before implementation.

If you plan to sell your business to your employees and have contracted to do so, be careful about subsequently changing your mind and selling to somebody else, even if you have the latitude to do so by contract. Your employees may depart, leaving you high and dry and effectively destroying the value of your organization.

A departing owner can be compensated for selling the business by several different methods, which can be used alone or in combination to produce benefits for the owner while allowing the employees to retain the business. Care must be taken to make sure the buyout arrangements are fair to both parties. These methods can help spread the payments over time, reducing the tax burden on the departing owner and the cash flow strain on the remaining employees or company. The various strategies include a direct sale of stock, stock redemptions, employment agreements, noncompete agreements, and consulting contracts. A combination plan may include a sale of owners' stock under an installment sale, along with consulting and noncompete agreements, to provide both buyer and seller with the best of all worlds.

The noncompete agreement compensates the departing owner in return for not starting up or obtaining employment in a competing business for an agreed upon period after the buyout. It usually also protects the employees and company from the owner soliciting the clients or employees of the firm. The noncompete agreement, like the installment sale, is usually structured so that the departing owner receives yearly payments over a five- to ten-year period. In addition, it is wise to use a consulting agreement to secure the departing owner's help in transitioning client relationships and transferring control of the business. The term of a consulting agreement varies, but is usually one to three years and compensates the owner in direct proportion to the level of services provided. These agreements, when used in combination, allow the owner to spread the proceeds of the sale over time, giving the owner the ability to spread the income and the recognition of gain over a longer period, resulting in less aggregate taxes on the transaction.

A Third-Party Sale

A significant number of older business owners will look to exit their businesses by selling to a third party. The larger institutional buyers like banks, brokerages, and insurance companies will buy some of these practices. However, most will probably be bought by relatively small organizations that are looking to increase local market share.

For example, in my case, I'm 45 years old. If I found somebody who was 60 years old who had a practice of similar size and quality and wanted to exit the business, I might be a likely acquirer. Just like any buyer, I would need to make sure that the terms were attractive by analyzing the likelihood of retaining clients and revenue through the key value drivers—client demographics, services being provided, and the quality of client relationships.

If you're going to sell to a third party, you need to ask yourself the same questions they are likely to ask you:

- Are you the key driver of value in your company?
- What are your responsibilities, duties, and tasks?
- Who are your key employees and what are their responsibilities, duties, and tasks?
- What happens when you leave?
- Who will take over your areas of responsibility?
- What is their demonstrated ability to perform these new responsibilities, and who will take over their existing responsibilities?
- Who provides advice and service to clients?
- Whom do clients identify as their advisor?
- Whom will they work with after you're gone?
- Can your business provide clients with a high level of service and satisfaction, ensuring continuity of revenue and profit, if you are not there?
- Explain in detail what would happen in your business if you were unable to go to work for a year?

Corporate structure recommendations: S vs C and voting and nonvoting capitalization to provide for control in governance and equity ownership by minority shareholders.

REGULATORY CONSIDERATIONS

You need to consider regulatory constraints for any type of transition or transaction. For example, if you're a fee-based money manager with accounts held at Schwab, and they find out that you have sold your business or that your designated control person has retired or died, they will remove your authorization to manage the accounts. The management authority rests in the control person designated for the Registered Investment Advisor (RIA) entity, not in the company itself. Your clients may be left without an investment manager, and your company will be left without the ability to manage and bill the accounts. That situation could be disastrous for your business, your clients, and the acquirer.

If you are affiliated with a broker-dealer, especially a wire-house, you don't own the client—they do. Even independent, financial planning broker-dealers still have to approve any succession planning you propose in advance, or they probably will not honor it. Your succession plan and buy-sell agreement should be approved and on file with your broker-dealer. As you can see, you must work ahead to make sure you stay within the regulatory framework in your industry; you should consider hiring a compliance professional to ensure compliance with all regulations.

BUY-SELL AGREEMENTS

A buy-sell agreement is a written agreement between co-owners of a business that details a plan allowing individual shareholders or the corporation to purchase the interest of a withdrawing or deceased shareholder. Buy-sell agreements usually obligate the departing shareholder to sell at a fixed price. The price may be a dollar amount or determined by a formula. Most agreements require that the value be reviewed and agreed on by all parties of interest to the agreement at least annually. Buy-sell agreements are important for the following reasons:

- Agreements provide a known purchaser for a departing shareholder's stock at a fair or agreed on price.
- Agreements provide liquidity for retirement or an owner's estate.

- Agreements prevent an unfriendly third party from acquiring the stock.
- Agreements eliminate friction between the surviving shareholders and the decedent's heirs.

Buy-sell agreements come in several flavors: cross purchase and stock redemption, as well as a hybrid that combines the best traits of each type of agreement. The hybrid agreement gives either the corporation or the shareholders a first option on all the departing shareholder's stock. The major advantage of a hybrid agreement is that it allows the various parties to determine which type of purchase would be most favorable at the time of purchase, based on tax considerations and the financial abilities of the corporation or shareholders to perform under the agreement. Regardless of the type, we would recommend using an independent trustee to control the agreement. The trustee ensures that all parties to the agreement perform as contemplated. If you have an insured buy-sell agreement to fund the death buyout of a key shareholder, then the trustee makes sure the stock of the deceased shareholder is exchanged for the insurance proceeds as planned. The trustee will make sure the agreement is implemented in the event a shareholder retires, dies prematurely, or becomes disabled. Prudence pays off. If you are depending on a buy-sell agreement to obtain or transfer the value of your most important asset, your business, then make sure you have an independent trustee to enforce the terms of your agreement.

EQUITY SHARING

If you're going to build a business that you will eventually sell or, in today's environment, even one that you will retain, you must provide some equity sharing to your employees. Employees love the Silicon Valley compensation model because they give stock options to their employees. If financial services organizations are to attract talented employees over the next ten years, they will need to offer the same type of equity plans.

Equity sharing plans are based on sharing stock in the company with selected or all employees. By providing employees with incentives based on the financial performance of the company's stock, equity plans encourage employees to work harder to ensure the financial success of the company. Because the economic benefit to the employee increases along with the value of the company's stock, these plans tie the interests of employees to the ultimate success of the company.

Several types of stock plans are worth consideration as equity-based compensation plans:

- *Incentive Stock Options (ISOs)*. This plan grants rights to employees to purchase shares of the corporation's stock at a certain price for a specified period of time. This is a qualified plan and is used to provide broad-based stock distribution, usually to all employees. Because ISOs are qualified, they have favorable tax treatment on exercise and sale.
- *Nonqualified Stock Options (NQSOs)*. This plan grants rights to employees to purchase shares of the corporation's stock at a certain price for a specified period of time. This is a nonqualified plan and is used to provide selective stock distribution to a few key employees. Because NQSOs are not qualified, they do not qualify for favorable tax treatment.
- *Nonqualified Discounted Stock Options (NQDSOs)*. NQDSOs are nonqualified stock options granting rights to selected employees to purchase shares of the corporation's stock at an exercise price that is considerably below fair market value of the underlying stock on the date of grant.
- *Employee Stock Purchase Plans (ESOPs)*. These plans provide employees with the right to purchase shares of the corporation's stock at fixed intervals, often through payroll deduction and at a discount. These plans are very popular with Fortune 500 companies and are used to provide broad dis-

tribution of stock to all employees. ESOPs are qualified plans and offer all employees an opportunity to purchase stock in the employer. ESOPs have been widely used by mid-size to large-size companies to redistribute ownership from a concentrated structure to broad-based ownership by all employees.

As businesses in our industry become larger, retaining good people can be a problem. We've found that, once trained, employees will often look for greener pastures. They look to make a move up to bigger organizations that can afford to pay more. Talented employees want to own a piece of the company through some type of equity sharing arrangement. We must be competitive in offering stock-based compensation plans to level the playing field.

Incentive-based stock option compensation is very popular today across all spectrums of industry and company size. These plans not only motivate employees to accomplish your strategic goals and objectives, but also ensure long-term retention of employees. By instituting an equity sharing arrangement, your employees will begin to think and act more like business owners, driving up the equity value of your company.

Sharing equity early with employees also allows you the flexibility to pick how you will retain or maximize the value of your owner's interest. If your employees have an equity stake, they will recognize that building value in the business depends on *their* performance, not just yours as business owner. This perception shift can really energize and drive value creation in the business, because your whole team is focused and motivated toward achieving business goals.

Without sharing equity, you will likely have a difficult time building significant equity value in your business. For example, let's say you decide you want to sell to employees over the next ten years. As time goes on, you're going to start to ease yourself into the background and take more vacations. If your employees don't have an equity stake, they may perceive that they get no credit for the value they are building in the business during this time period. They are likely to become disenchanted with the idea of buying a business for top dollar at the end of the ten years, when they are in fact building and enhancing the value today. Chances are they'll leave, and you have nothing to sell if you can't keep your employees.

The solution? Share equity today and over time that directly reflects employees' relative contribution to increased profits and value in your company. When you share equity, you must give your employees a way to measure the value of their equity interest. We use our valuation model to value our business each year. Because we are not publicly traded, this model is the only way to measure value creation, goal achievement, and employee contributions. Our nonqualified stock option plan for key employees allows us to provide incentive-based compensation that does not impact current cash flow. It also has been a key driver of growth, as these employees have been energized to accomplish our strategic goals. We are also evaluating a companywide Incentive Stock Option Plan, which would allow all employees to participate and "get a piece of the rock."

To share equity, especially stock options, a small company doesn't need to have open book accounting, but I think employees should understand the company's financial health, profitability, and the factors that drive equity value. You need to be able to share with employees how the company's strategic and financial goals translate to higher equity value and increased opportunities for higher compensation.

As a simple example, over the past year, our office supply expenses have doubled, but our employee base certainly hasn't. At our strategic planning update meeting, we explained that the more often employees shop in Staples catalogs for pens, pencils, and this and that, the less likely we would be able to compensate hardworking, diligent employees at the end of the year—we will have spent the profit required to provide employees with increases. Not surprisingly, office supply expenses have fallen back into line with budgeted expenditures. Our employees would much rather receive increases in compensation than equip themselves with six colors of sticky notes.

Equity sharing definitely has some problems, but I don't see any way around it. Owners often fear sharing equity for a variety of reasons, but most centers around control. One of the main reasons people start their own businesses is to control their destiny; sharing equity feels like giving up control. The reason we created both a voting and nonvoting class of stock was to reduce these concerns. Employees participate in the equity and value creation of the business by owning nonvoting stock, while the owners maintain control through voting stock. In our case we decided to recapitalize our company, providing for both voting and nonvoting common stock. We were able to reduce the control concerns of the major shareholders by using nonvoting stock as the funding vehicle for our nonqualified stock option plan.

As the company gains in size, momentum, and number of employees, the second step is a broader based incentive stock option plan where everybody gets some options on shares. Our dilemma is an ethical one that centers on our ability as owners to create value for all shareholders. We have established a nonqualified stock option plan for executives and key manager positions, vested over a five-year period. At this point, we've allocated 25 percent of the equity in the company to our employees under this plan, and we've reserved another 15 percent for a qualified incentive stock option plan for broad-based employee ownership.

The problem with distributing equity ownership of any type is that if the business itself never gains the size and credibility to become significantly valuable, then these options have negligible value and can become a disincentive. For stock-based compensation to motivate, the stock has to increase in value over time. The company has to grow big enough to go public or to ensure an acquisition that will maximize the value of all shareholders' interest. Most companies don't go public unless they have at least three years of profitable earnings growth and $100 million in revenues. Few, if any, financial planning companies will grow this large, so planning to be acquired would seem the more logical strategy.

Determining the right equity-sharing plan is a complex decision and should only be undertaken with the advice of appropriate advisors. Senior management needs to participate with an attorney experienced in corporate reorganizations and qualified and non-qualified stock plans, and with an accountant familiar with the company's finances and the impact of these plans on the company's financial status.

Summary

We are at the point in our industry's lifecycle where accelerating competition, advances in technology, and large, well-capitalized competitors are unleashing such competitive force on the old *sales practice business model* that it will cease to be competitive. This change is like a hammer hitting a rock with great force. Pieces don't just break off in one direction—the rock is completely pulverized, exploding in all directions. The only question in the minds of those that study the industry is: How long will it be before sales practices start to die out, eventually ceasing to exist altogether? It seems that we can either evolve by reengineering our sales practice business model, or risk extinction.

We can start to evolve by changing the old models and by not repeating the same old mistakes. It is time to turn weakness into strength and our mistakes into winning strategies:

- *Winning Strategy #1.* We have institutionalized our organization and our relationships with our clients. No one person is the focal point; advice and service are provided by the entire organization. By shifting the focus of advice and service to our organization, we gained a wonderful benefit—clients received better advice and service, while our life became more enjoyable and manageable.

- *Winning Strategy #2.* We focus our energies and sales effort to capture recurring revenue stream, which provides our firm with more predictable cash flow. Recurring revenue supports expansion programs and increases profitability, in turn leading to higher compensation for employees and shareholders.

- *Winning Strategy #3.* We reinvest in ourselves, channeling profits back into the business to support infrastructure expansion and growth. Businesses require capital to compete effectively, so we establish a systematic capital retention program to build a reserve, allowing the company to be its own banker.

- *Winning Strategy #4.* We recognize the risk inherent in building any business, so we separate our personal and business assets. We recognize that industries, competition, and the business environment are always in a state of flux, which inherently creates risk for the business owner. Business value is relative; just because a business is valuable today does not mean that it will be valuable in the future. With adequate capital, the business can fund expansion and short-term cash flow crunches without dipping into the owners' personal assets.

- *Winning Strategy #5.* Having recognized that our business was only a tool to facilitate our personal vision, we use our written vision statement as the foundation for developing a written strategic business plan. We make sure our personal objectives and goals come first and the needs of the business second.

- *Winning Strategy #6.* We carefully identify our target markets and determine our best client profile and then institute an effective marketing plan based on our unique selling proposition. We supercharge our marketing effort by developing a credibility marketing plan to build brand awareness and become recognized as an expert.

- *Winning Strategy #7*. We know exactly what our target clients want—an advisory relationship based on solving client problems through a comprehensive financial plan. Comprehensive planning and ongoing turnkey management of all the clients' financial affairs is the affluent consumer's preference. Through comprehensive planning, we keep the client focused on achieving long-term goals, not on daily market gyrations and short-term investment performance. Client-specific planning and customized financial solutions are difficult, if not impossible, for larger competitors to mass produce, providing us with a competitive advantage.
- *Winning Strategy #8*. We develop a written strategic business plan to guide company operations, making the plan come to life in our organization by adopting a strategic management process. Executive management and employees become focused on accomplishing the company's strategic objective and goals, providing everyone with a great sense of accomplishment and personal fulfillment.
- *Winning Strategy #9*. We formalize our partnering relationships with others to implement our business plans more effectively. We share our business plan with our resource partners-custodians, broker-dealers, and product companies to channel their resources more effectively. We create formal joint ventures with accountants, attorneys, and other professionals acting as a catalyst, facilitating their entry into the financial services business. Our institutional quality business model provides the foundation for collaboration, revenue sharing, and unparalleled growth.
- *Winning Strategy #10*. We have developed a uniform advice and service platform while standardizing practices through written standard operating procedures. We harness technology to create capacity, providing more clients with an outstanding level of advice and service and turning them into referral advocates. By shifting service and advice away from individual planners to our organization, we experi-

ence a wonderful side benefit—planners' lives become more manageable and enjoyable.

- *Winning Strategy #11.* We adopt a formal financial management system focusing on cash flow management to ensure that our business plan is based on accurate financial projections. Balancing growth plans and financial resources is critically important to achieving success.
- *Winning Strategy #12.* As part of developing our personal vision statement and business plan, we determine an exit strategy and create a valuation model to track our progress toward building shareholder value. Most of us will retire, sell, or exit our business at some time in the future, and we will need a plan to maximize value for shareholders, while providing continuity for employees and clients.

Remember that all strategies need to be integrated into a written business plan. There are good ideas and bad ideas. Each idea needs to be measured against the company's strategic objective and goals to determine if it is worthy of inclusion in the plan. If you fail to measure each new idea against the integrated strategy documented in your business plan, you will probably stray off course and never complete your mission. The idea of *Best Practices* being promoted from the podium at many industry conferences can be dangerous unless the best practice improves your existing strategy.

Our industry is in a state of extreme flux, evolving rapidly along several clear lines of competitive demarcation as all competitors vie for control of the affluent consumer marketplace:

- Comprehensive financial planning and turnkey financial management delivered through a trusted advisor and based on a face-to-face relationship.
- A modular product and service offering helping the affluent consumer make educated decisions regarding their financial futures. Delivered through portals utilizing sophisticated technology tools to create an environment through which all client financial activities can be facilitated.

- A hybrid approach that uses the best of technology to support the trusted advisor relationship, providing advice and service offerings based on financial planning fundamentals.

You must recognize the dynamic changes recasting the competitive landscape of our industry and decide how your organization will compete effectively. This is the million-dollar question that each of us must answer for ourselves. Luckily, it need not be your final answer. Business planning is a dynamic process that needs to be updated to reflect the changes taking place in the industry and your personal life.

To determine how you can compete effectively, review Part Three of this book, *Engineering a Business Plan*. This section outlines a step-by-step guide to creating your personal vision statement and written business plan. It will help you answer these tough questions about how to compete effectively, how to create equity, and eventually how to successfully exit your business.

Remember your personal vision of what you want your life to be is the anchor of this whole process and will determine if you will succeed in attaining your goals and dreams. (A sample strategic operating business plan can be found in Appendix D.)

Converting your sales practice into a world-class business requires focus, determination, and the ability to adopt a strategic management process through which to channel your daily business efforts and implement your strategy. This process will help you decide what you want out of life and how your business can help you get it. It will help you achieve your goals, as well as the goals of your clients and employees. Everyone around you will benefit, and at the end of the day you will have a business with significant equity value and an exit strategy to capitalize on it.

In Part 4 of the book, Institutionalizing Your Business, you learn how to up your game by adding winning strategies to your business plan. You can convert your sales practice into an institutional quality business by creating uniform service platforms based on standard operating procedures, allowing your organization to provide unparalleled service.

Converting Your Practice into a World-Class Business

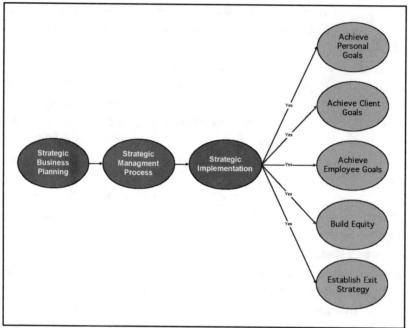

You will also find sections on how to build a job description program, a performance appraisal system, and a salary administration program in the Appendix. These human resource tools will allow you to focus your employees' efforts to accomplish your business strategy. You will also find a process and technology overview detailing some of the tools we have developed to help us upgrade our business model.

All of these tools will allow you to systematize your business and supercharge your organization to provide a higher quality of service to more clients, which in turn will enable you to increase the size and scale of your business. You will not only compete with the big firms, but you can win the battle for affluent clients.

I realized years ago that I had a choice. I could go to work every day and earn a great living by providing planning services to clients, or I could *focus my energies on building a great business with significant value* while earning a great living by providing planning services to clients. You have the same choice. If you follow the planning prescriptions outlined in the book, you will be able to build a business that will provide your clients with better advice and service, your employees with a more rewarding career and an opportunity to be financially successful, you with a better quality of life, and, at the end of the day, a business with tremendous equity value.

As the competition heats up our industry, the challenges become great, but that only makes the game worth playing. Best of luck building your own world-class enterprise.

The American Dream

The Dream = Reality
You control your destiny.
You have personal freedom.
Your business has significant equity value.
You have achieved financial independence.

APPENDIX A

Building a Job Description Program

The key to using a strategic management process to manage your company is making your business plan come to life. You will know that you are actually managing your organization to accomplish your strategic objective and goals when you can measure everything you and your employees do during each day against the dictates of your plan. You must tie performance measurement and goal accomplishment together in your human resources platform. This will focus your employees to accomplish your company's strategy, objective, and goals. Communicating your company goals, defining areas of responsibility, and establishing performance criteria are critical to your success. The following chart demonstrates how your human resources platform ties it all together.

What is a job description?

A job description is a concise statement of the responsibilities, duties, tasks, and relationships built into a job. The description outlines the requirements for performing the work, its frequency, and its scope. It is based on the nature of the work and *not* on the individual currently performing it.

Why are job description programs needed?

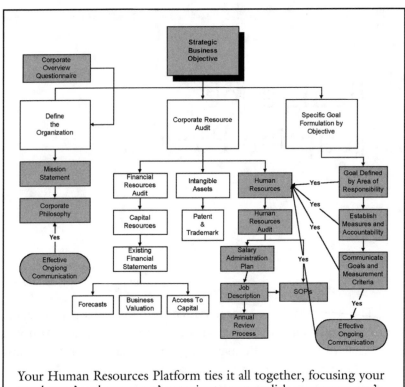

Your Human Resources Platform ties it all together, focusing your employees' and managers' energies to accomplish your company's strategy, objective, and goals.

To manage effectively, managers must be able to identify the work that needs to be performed, then delegate it to others and control its progress and accomplishments. They need definitions of the various tasks, duties, responsibilities, and relationships of all members of the work group. In addition, the way any organization operates can be improved by using job descriptions for assigning responsibility, delegating authority, and identifying individual duties.

A number of problems can usually be solved by creating a job description program. They include:

- Inadequate, inequitable, or inconsistent pay practices
- Complaints from employees that they do not know or feel comfortable with their job responsibilities
- Frequent conflicts and misunderstandings about who is supposed to do what
- Overlapping responsibilities and duties that result in duplication of effort
- Selection and hiring of people who are not qualified for their jobs
- Inadequate or poor training that leads to poor productivity, low quality, and low morale
- Complaints from employees about being overwhelmed, not being able to complete tasks, or feeling overloaded
- Delays in production of financial planning advice or services

Good job descriptions help in compensating, selecting, and hiring of personnel; design of jobs; conducting performance appraisals; and workflow planning.

What are the benefits of job descriptions?

Job descriptions are used to compare one job to another and to detail key responsibilities, duties, and tasks by function for specific jobs. This kind of analysis also allows managers to evaluate jobs for compensation purposes and wage and salary administration, and it ensures consistency in setting pay rates among individual workers and groups of employees.

Properly drawn job descriptions can help in the recruitment, selection, and hiring of new employees by allowing managers to spell out the exact qualifications, education, skills, and experience a new hire needs to be successful. They help direct the questions interviewers will ask job applicants by focusing only on relevant facts pertaining to the job. In addition, job descriptions help growing companies plan future manpower needs by comparing current workflow requirements with those jobs and skills expected to be required in the future. Training programs are developed and administered with the help of job descriptions. Measuring employee performance against accomplishment of the responsibilities, duties, and tasks outlined in the job description should be the basis for periodic formal appraisals. Ideally, job descriptions should integrate departmental as well as company goals to focus each employee's efforts toward goal achievement.

Job descriptions can also be instrumental in planning or changing workflow patterns. They can be used to help construct workflow diagrams, which in turn may uncover tasks that have been overlooked in describing certain jobs. By carefully reviewing job descriptions, managers can resolve workflow overloads and prevent employee burnout.

What kind of information should be included in a job description?

Experts agree that the style, content, and form for job descriptions should include:

- *Job title, organizational unit, accountability.* These items identify the job and give it unique characteristics.
- *Job summary.* This defines work to be performed and summarizes in three or four sentences the functions for which the position has been delegated responsibility and authority. It states the overall objective of the position, what the position does, the reason for doing it, and its intended result. Two job descriptions with the same title and same level of pay may have differing responsibilities, duties, and tasks.
- *Duties and tasks.* This part of the job description describes the task to be performed.
- *Skill and educational requirements.* Describe the skills needed, educational requirements, special training, and amount of experience needed.
- *Interrelationships.* This specifies the relationships between the job and other jobs in the organization, especially reporting and supervisory relationships.
- *Management flexibility statement.* An example might be:

The above information has been designed to indicate the general nature and level of work performed by employees within this classification. It is not designed to contain or be interpreted as a comprehensive inventory of all duties, responsibilities, and qualifications required of employees assigned to this job.

What is the best way to gain employee cooperation when starting a job description program?

Top management must support the program and clearly communicate that support. Such communication should include these key elements:

- The primary reasons for establishing the program
- The individual or group responsible for its development
- The units of the company covered by the program
- The procedure for reviewing drafts of the job descriptions

JOB DESCRIPTION WORKSHEET

1. Job identification

   (a) Name of organizational unit _____

   (b) Current job title _____

   (c) Location _____

   (d) Direct supervisor _____

2. Complete Responsibilities, Duties, and Tasks (RDT) Worksheet

   (a) Specific, frequently performed tasks

   _____

   (b) Responsibilities

   _____

3. State specific job requirements: education, knowledge, degrees, or certification

   (a) Education

   _____

   (b) Knowledge

   _____

   (c) Certification

   _____

   (d) Experience

   _____

4. How skills are acquired: school, special courses, experience, or training

   _____

5. Special requirements (describe)

   (a) Travel _____

   (b) Long hours _____

   (c) Other _____

6. Goals (describe)

   (a) Employee _____

   (b) Departmental _____

   (c) Company _____

Getting Results through Performance Appraisal

What are the objectives of a good performance appraisal system? When selecting an appraisal system for your company, your first concern should be to set the standards for accurate and fair performance reviews. The criteria against which you judge an employee must be clearly related to the responsibilities, duties, and tasks assigned to the job. The process must be as objective as you can make it. In general, objectivity in performance appraisal is possible only when following a fundamental rule: Judge the quality and quantity of work, not the person or personality.

An objective evaluation system will help your company to:

- Eliminate uneven standards from manager to manager. For example, one manager may prize employees who are flexible, cooperative, and likeable and rank them very highly. Another manager might not consider people skills or personality important at all.
- Remove the temptation to judge employees by their personalities. When every manager ranks employees by the same specific standards, appraisals can focus on qualities that are

related to job performance, not on whether a manager likes or dislikes an employee.

- Motivate employees with appraisals. Employees know that appraisals form the basis of many important promotion and salary decisions. When employees believe they are judged fairly, they will respect the system and view appraisals as a way to improve their performance.
- Create the most productive work force possible. Using appraisal standards that are objective and measurable ensures that managers recognize and reward employees for skills that further the goals and profits of the company.

What appraisal methods are available? Several basic ways are available to appraise employees. Some of the most popular include:

- The rating scale system, in which the employee is given a numerical score for each item on a list of job-related performance characteristics. The characteristics are based on job requirements.
- The behavior scale, which assigns a number value to job-related behavior, such as whether an employee's daily work habits are consistent or how well employees respond to deadline pressure.
- The essay appraisal, which uses a narrative style
- Appraisals that are part of your management by objective program. After stating the job's objectives, the appraisal determines how successfully the individual reached them.

These classifications are primarily for purposes of illustration. In practice, we have integrated most combinations or variations of these basic types into one appraisal system.

When are rating scales the best appraisal method? The key to success with a rating scale is to select the right characteristics on which to evaluate an employee and a scale with which to rate them. Many companies start by establishing a scale of one to five, such as:

1. Exceptional
2. Above average
3. Average
4. Needs improvement
5. Unsatisfactory

They rate each employee according to that scale. Commonly used factors are quality and quantity of work, cooperation, initiative, planning, and leadership abilities. Then they rate them on goal accomplishment as it relates to fulfilling their responsibilities and accomplishing their duties and tasks. Finally, they rate the employee on their effort toward achieving the strategic goals of their department and the company.

How does the *management-by-objectives* (MBO) *approach* fit with performance appraisals? Management-by-objectives is the well-known technique of setting goals, then judging how well they are met. Performance appraisal is a major part of that process. The supervisor and the employee establish stated objectives the employee should reach by the end of the rating period. Then the appraisal becomes a simple matter of deciding how well the employee met those goals. The key to this method's success is to clearly define the goals, then accompany each one with specific standards that measure success.

The major advantage of the MBO system is that it offers a structure for the employee and guidance to the supervisor when rating the employee. Employees know in advance exactly what is expected of them. They also know they will be judged by accomplishing their objectives.

An effective plan requires that the supervisor and the employee agree on the proper objectives. Both must have the time to discuss and negotiate these goals before the rating period starts. Goals are established at the beginning of the year or on the employee's anniversary. Also, the plan must include a provision to modify goals that become clearly impossible to meet or when certain milestones are achieved. We recommend updating an employee's review at least semiannually.

The first step in setting those criteria is to look at the company's overall goals and those of the particular department, then decide on what must be expected of the individual so the department can meet its objectives.

The employee's role at this stage is critical to the success of its appraisal program. The employee and supervisor draw up a list of performance goals for the job, usually for a period of six months. This list should encompass all of the major areas of the job. The goals should be challenging, representing improvements over previous accomplishments. They should be realistic and attainable within the time frame selected.

Whenever possible, goal statements should be accompanied by a specific date for completion and include the level of performance to be attained. Thus, "to gather more assets" is not sufficient as a goal statement. A better goal statement would be "to increase asset gathering by 20 percent per year, to $5 million new assets by December 31."

How should you prepare for the appraisal interview? The appraisal form has two parts: Part A, the supervisor's form; and Part B, the employee's form. The employee should review and fill out Part B and return it to the supervisor before the interview.

Sample Performance Appraisal Plan

**Instructions for Completing
Employee Performance Appraisal**

The Employee Performance Appraisal Form consists of two parts:

Form A. Form A is to be completed by the employee's immediate supervisor. The supervisor should solicit comments about the employee from the supervisor's upper level manager and from those employees who regularly interface with the employee. Recognize, however, that the employee is not being reviewed by peers, but by the supervisor. Therefore, the comments received from others should help support and/or reaffirm an opinion about the employee's performance, not be the sole basis on which a particular area of performance is graded.

The appraisal consists of eight major areas of performance. Within each major area are several descriptions of skills or work qualities that help define the employee's performance. The supervisor is to score the employee in each skill or quality based on the level of the employee's performance. Skills that are not applicable to an employee's performance or job function need not be scored and should be so marked.

The average of all skills will determine the overall performance grade of the appraisal. The supervisor may also average the scores within each major area to determine areas of strength and/or weakness.

Once the supervisor has completed the appraisal, it should be submitted to a next level supervisor for final review and comment before giving it to the employee.

Form B. Form B is to be given to the employee two weeks prior to their anniversary date and must be returned to the supervisor within one week.

The employee must be given the opportunity to read and review their performance appraisal for at least two days prior to the formal review meeting with a supervisor. This will give them the opportunity to gather their thoughts so that they are prepared to discuss the content of their review.

Employee Performance Appraisal

Employee: _____ Review Date: _____

Review Period: _____ to _____ Position: _____

(continued)

Job Class: _____ Hire Date: _____

Reason for Appraisal:

____Annual ____ Promotion ____ Merit ____ Transfer
____ Probation ____ Other

General Performance Review

Circle the number in the right hand column that most accurately reflects the employee's performance. If an item does not apply to the job being reviewed, put a line through the item.

1—always (outstanding) 2—almost always (good) 3—usually (average) 4—sometimes (needs improvement) 5—never (unsatisfactory)

Quality of Work:

Work is accurate.	1	2	3	4	5
Work is neat and well presented.	1	2	3	4	5
Work is carefully planned.	1	2	3	4	5
Work is well organized and thorough.	1	2	3	4	5
Checks work carefully as required.	1	2	3	4	5

Productivity:

Works quickly.	1	2	3	4	5
High level of production.	1	2	3	4	5
Willingly works overtime when necessary.	1	2	3	4	5
Uses time well.	1	2	3	4	5
Handles pressure.	1	2	3	4	5
Meets deadlines.	1	2	3	4	5
Achieves balance between quality and quantity.	1	2	3	4	5

Organization Skills:

Keeps track of work items.	1	2	3	4	5
Accurately prioritizes work.	1	2	3	4	5
Adjusts easily to changing priorities.	1	2	3	4	5
Manages large, complex priorities.	1	2	3	4	5
Organizes people to reach goals.	1	2	3	4	5

Knowledge of Job:

Knows where to go to get information.	1	2	3	4	5
Used as a source of information by others.	1	2	3	4	5
Understands processes involved in getting work out.	1	2	3	4	5
Knows where to refer others when necessary.	1	2	3	4	5

Communication:

Listens carefully to what others say.	1	2	3	4	5
Asks for clarification when necessary.	1	2	3	4	5
Responses to others indicate understanding.	1	2	3	4	5
Expresses ideas so others understand.	1	2	3	4	5
Communicates work status or problems to supervisor.	1	2	3	4	5

Interpersonal Skills:

Is sought out by others for advice.	1	2	3	4	5
Cooperates with others at work to get job done.	1	2	3	4	5
Shows tact and courtesy with others.	1	2	3	4	5
Deals calmly with others.	1	2	3	4	5
Handles questions or requests from others in a helpful manner.	1	2	3	4	5
Maintains good work relations within and outside company.	1	2	3	4	5
Handles criticism.	1	2	3	4	5
Takes responsibility for actions.	1	2	3	4	5

Need for Supervision:

Can be relied on to get work done without supervision.	1	2	3	4	5
Can direct or instruct others about work.	1	2	3	4	5
Takes initiative when appropriate.	1	2	3	4	5
Asks for additional work when has free time.	1	2	3	4	5

(continued)

Problem Solving:

Recognizes problems.	1	2	3	4	5
Collects relevant data to solve problems.	1	2	3	4	5
Solves problems quickly.	1	2	3	4	5
Solves problems accurately.	1	2	3	4	5
Knows when to ask advice from the right person.	1	2	3	4	5
Seeks out methods to do the job more efficiently.	1	2	3	4	5

Absenteeism:

Number of unexplained and/or unacceptable absences during review period _____

Total number of sick days this calendar year _____

Number of sick days over the limit this year _____

Warning required? Yes _____ No _____

Warning given? Yes _____ No _____

Lateness:

Number of days late for work during review period _____

Warning required? Yes _____ No _____

Warning given? Yes _____ No _____

Comments:

_____

_____

_____

_____

Major Duties and Responsibilities:

List the major duties of the job in order of importance and record any established measurement standards. Then rate performance and comment on each duty. This area can also be used for written comments on accomplishments or guidance concerning improvements needed.

Major Duties, Responsibilities, Goals, and Measurements	Performance Rating and Comments
1.	
2.	
3.	
4.	
5.	
6.	

Development Planning:

Use the rating and review in the previous sections in completing Items 1 and 2. Use the employee's responses to the questions on Form B to complete Item 3.

1. Strengths:
   a) What two or three things were done exceptionally well in this review period?

   b) How will the employee's skills be used to maximum advantage?

2. Improvements:
   a) What two or three things could have been done better?

   b) What action steps will be taken to help the employee improve in these areas?

(continued)

3. Career Development:
   a) What are the employee's stated performance-related goals and objectives?

   b) What are the supervisor's goals and objectives for the employee?

   c) What are the employee's stated career goals?

   d) What action steps are to be taken to accomplish the above?

General Comments/Overall Performance Summary:

_____

_____

_____

_____

_____

Overall Performance Grade: _____

Grade Descriptions:

Grade 1: Performance significantly exceeds expectations in all major areas and is considered outstanding. Individual has demonstrated ability to exceed performance objectives on a sustained basis.

Grade 2: Performance fully meets expectations in all major areas of responsibility and exceeds expectations in some areas.

Grade 3: Performance meets minimum expectations and is considered average. Areas of weakness resulting in an overall average score offset areas of strength. Some objectives were achieved, but not in a fully satisfactory manner. Areas of improvement are needed.

Grade 4: Performance does not meet overall minimum expectations and is considered poor. While performance may meet expectations in a few areas, the majority of important responsibilities are not being performed at the expected level. A probationary period may be extended or initiated at the discretion of the individual's immediate supervisor. A Grade 4 performance may result in termination for an employee already on probation.

Grade 5: Performance is significantly below expectations for an individual with similar training and time on the job and is considered unsatisfactory. A mandatory 90-day probationary period is initiated. A Grade 5 performance may result in termination for an employee already on probation.

Compensation Review:

Current Salary: _____ Proposed Increase: _____

New Salary: _____ Effective Date: _____

The above evaluation has been reviewed with me:

Employee Signature: _____ Date: _____

I have discussed the above evaluation with the employee:

Supervisor Signature: _____ Date: _____

Upper Level Manager: _____ Date: _____

Employee Comments: Name: _____

1. What do you consider to be your strengths? How do they fit with your current job?

2. What do you see as your limitations, if any? How do they keep you from achieving your potential?

3. What would you like your next career step to be? Where do you see yourself going with the company? By when?

(continued)

4. What can your supervisor or the company do to help you improve your performance and achieve your goals?

5. Are there any other problems or concerns you would like to discuss with your supervisor?

Employee Signature: _____ Date: _____

Exit Performance Appraisal

Submit all supporting documents including the letter of resignation to the Human Resources Department prior to:

_____ Termination _____ Transfer _____ Leave

Name: _____ Position Number/Title: _____

Department: _____

Date of Hire: _____ Last Day of Work: _____

1. State the reason for the termination, transfer or leave.

   Check and explain _____ Voluntary _____ Involuntary

   _____

2. Evaluate the quality and quantity of work produced by the employee.

   _____

3. Comment on the employee's behavior in relating to fellow employees and supervisors.

   _____

4. If termination, is replacement needed?

   _____ Yes   _____ No   Date: _____

Overall Assessment of Performance:

Unsatisfactory Peformance	Performance Needs to Improve	Fully Meetss Requirements	Consistently Exceeds Requirements	Distinguished Performance
1	2	3	4	5

Supervisor's explanation of rating:

_____

_____

Supervisor: _____ Date: _____

Manager: _____ Date: _____

Why should supervisors and managers be trained in performance appraisals? Training helps supervisors and managers use uniform methods of appraisal throughout the organization. Training also reduces biases, promotes accuracy, and stimulates participation in the system.

Effective performance appraisal training almost always involves modeling and role-playing. There's no standard method for conducting a performance appraisal interview because each employee is unique. Supervisors and managers will learn best by observing model interviews and by receiving feedback.

Every year when our strategic plan is updated, each manager must set departmental goals to guide all employees in his or her department to accomplish the strategic goals outlined in the plan. At the beginning of each year, managers outline departmental goals and performance standards, and set each employee's area of responsibility. These assignments are used to update each employee's job description. Each employee then has a complete understanding of the goals and the performance measurement criteria that will be used to rate her or him over the next performance period.

Summary of Department Goals

Department: _____   Manager: _____

Period: _____

GOAL	PERFORMANCE STANDARD	RESPONSIBLE EMPLOYEE	TO BE MET BY (DATE)
_____	_____	_____	_____
_____	_____	_____	_____
_____	_____	_____	_____
_____	_____	_____	_____
_____	_____	_____	_____
_____	_____	_____	_____
_____	_____	_____	_____
_____	_____	_____	_____
_____	_____	_____	_____
_____	_____	_____	_____
_____	_____	_____	_____

Unfortunately, from time to time employees will leave your firm, either of their own volition or because you have encouraged them to look elsewhere for employment. When employees leave it is important to conduct exit interviews. Departing employees often will be very candid about problems that may exist in your company. You can determine why they leave and/or why they were not successful in your organization. This will help you gain useful information to evaluate the success of your training programs and performance appraisal systems.

Developing an Effective Wage and Salary Administration Program

What are the main purposes of a compensation system? The main goals of a sound compensation system are to attract, hold, and motivate good employees. Such a program will establish positive links between an individual's pay and their performance. Other purposes include eliminating morale problems caused by inequitable pay, giving your firm a good reputation, improving the quality of employees' performance, and raising their productivity level.

How are job descriptions used in compensation programs? The job and position descriptions provide the basic information about the tasks, duties, responsibilities, and working environment so the Evaluation Committee can successfully complete its efforts to rank, rate, and set money values on jobs.

What approaches can be used to rate the value of jobs? Evaluation of jobs is not an exact science. The members of the Evaluation Committee can reduce subjectivity, though, by requiring its members to reach unanimity on the values of jobs. Though the chief executive's job is clearly worth more than, say, a clerk's, when you look at jobs or positions that are more closely related, the differences are not so obvious. Most firms use one of these two approaches:

1. *The market value approach.* This approach produces an evaluation of your company's jobs and positions by comparing your company's wages and salaries with those paid by other firms. Recently, the Financial Planning Association (FPA) completed a compensation study, which provides owners of financial planning organizations accurate wage and salary information for making comparisons.

2. *The internal value approach.* This approach evaluates the firm's jobs and positions by making careful internal com-

Job Class Salary Ranges / Job Class Assignments

Job Class		Range Low to High	Overlap	Span	Job Class Assignments
1	a	100k to 250k	25k	50k	Executive VP, President, CEO
2	a	75k to 125k	0k	50k	Vice-President, Director, Senior Planner
	b	55k to 75k	5k	20k	Manager of Operations, Planning
	c	45k to 60k	5k	15k	Supervisor, Associate Planner
3	a	40k to 50k	2k	10k	Planning Specialist, Operations Specialist
	b	35k to 42k	3k	7k	Planning Assistant, Operations Assistant
	c	30k to 38	3k	8k	Administrative Specialist, Bookkeeper
4	a	26k to 33k	4k	7k	Secretary
	b	24k to 30k	4k	6k	Receptionist
	c	20k to 28k	4k	8k	File and Shipping Supervisor
5	a	18k to 24k	2k	6k	File Clerk
	b	16k to 20k	n/a	4k	Part Time Administrative
	c	N/A			

parisons between jobs and ranking them in proportion to their value to the firm.

Many firms use a combination of approaches to temper the results of data gathered by others. We identify salary ranges for administration by job class, then assign various jobs to each class. This process allows management to rank jobs according to contribution to the company and establish fair standards for pay and promotion increases.

A SAMPLE STRATEGIC BUSINESS PLAN

Anne's Financial Group, Inc. (AFG)

Date: January 1, 1999

This document is confidential and is intended for use by AFG's employees only. Any distribution of this document will violate the company's confidentiality program.

TABLE OF CONTENTS

PERSONAL VISION PLANNING

Remember that even if you've been in business for years, Personal Vision Planning will help you determine whom you really want to be, where you really want to go, and what you really want to accomplish in your life. Your personal vision statements are the foundation for creating a strategic business plan that will guide your company operations and ultimately ensure you accomplish your personal goals. Your personal goals are the priority, not the business. The business is only a vehicle to *facilitate* accomplishing your personal goals.

The strategic business plan illustration that follows is the plan that Anne developed to convert her sales practice, which was robbing her of everything important to her in her personal life, into a business that would allow her to achieve her personal goals. Her personal vision statements are the foundation for developing her plan.

The Founder's Personal Vision Planning Goals

- To spend quality time daily with her children
- To spend more quality time with her husband
- To make a significant contribution of her time to her church and the community
- To exercise daily
- To enrich her life by actually taking at least three vacations per year and traveling abroad
- To continue to live in her family's home
- To spend as many weekends at their shore home as possible
- To continue to send her children to private schools
- To be financially independent within ten years

The Founder's Personal Financial Goals

- Continue to maintain current lifestyle spending of $15,000 per month after taxes

- Be able to retire within ten years, with targeted spendable retirement income of $12,000 per month adjusted for inflation
- Provide $30,000 per year (adjusted for inflation) per child in college education funding
- Be able to sell the business within three to five years
- Anne's personal retirement analysis indicates that she is dependent on selling the business to help fund her retirement.

The Founder's Personal Life Goals at Work

- After some extensive soul searching, she indicated she would be willing to work no more than five days a week, eight hours a day for the next year. After which, she would be willing to work only four days a week during the second year, after which she would be willing to work only three days a week.
- She wants to be in a position to sell the business or walk away, retaining an income interest for three to five years.
- She wants to concentrate on what she enjoys doing most, which is working with clients to solve their financial problems.
- Anne does not want to get involved in the day-to-day management of her practice and has decided to hire someone to run the practice for her and to add additional management support to ease her other responsibilities as well.
- She would like to be able to sell her business for about two times revenue to help fund her retirement goals.

THE COMPANY

Company History

Anne started her career in the financial industry in 1986 with a large brokerage firm. Seeing the increasing need and opportunity to provide financial planning advice, Anne successfully completed a CFP program, obtaining her designation in 1989. Over the next few years, she began developing a practice that concentrated on retiring executives being downsized from large corporations.

In 1992, Anne left the brokerage business to begin a family and to start a financial planning business in her home, part-time, offering services to some existing clients who continued to call her for advice. She felt that she would have the ideal job, working from her home part-time while being able to spend quality time with her family.

Funding for her new business came from savings, she committed $10,000 to set up her practice. Anne continued to increase her hours as the practice expanded, and shortly after having her second child, Anne moved her business to an office several miles from her home. In 1994, Anne hired her first staff person, Matt, a CFP, as planning manager to help her with writing plans and back office operations. As her client base continued to grow, Anne found herself working more and more hours. To ease her burden, she hired several additional staff people: Judy as planning administrator, Debbie as secretary, and Jennifer as a receptionist.

In 1996 Anne incorporated as Anne's Financial Group, Inc. (AFG), a Subchapter "S" corporation, to formalize her business structure. By 1998 she had about 300 clients with $60,000,000 invested in various load-based mutual funds. Recently, she has started to move her clients to fee-based programs, recognizing the need to have a recurring source of revenue to help support and build her practice.

Because she has concentrated on retirement planning, Anne has been able to work with about 60 new clients per year, obtained mostly through referrals from existing clients and executive retirement planning seminars held at a few large communications companies located in her town. She has developed several key contacts, from client referrals, within the human resources departments at these companies, who routinely ask her to provide seminars for retiring or downsized executives. Anne has continued to increase her knowledge of retirement transition planning issues and feels that other professionals, especially brokers, cannot effectively compete with her for this business.

Anne feels that she has reached a critical stage in her business career as her personal and business life have become unmanageable. She has decided to not only limit the number of new clients she will work with, but also wants to change her practice so it is less dependent on her to do everything.

The Company's Mission

We will develop advisory relationships based on comprehensive financial planning, providing retirement advice and investment management to clients, which will enable them to achieve their retirement goals.

Corporate Philosophy

- We need to always place our client's interests first.
- We need to add tangible value to each client situation by helping them achieve their financial goals.
- We will strive to provide the highest quality advice available in the retirement planning field.
- We need to attract and retain talented people.
- We need to grow and earn a reasonable profit to ensure that we can keep our advisory commitment to our clients.
- We need to provide excellent opportunity for our employees.

INDUSTRY ANALYSIS

AFG provides clients with value-added advice and service focusing on retirement planning and benefits coordination planning. Our goal is to provide a complete spectrum of products and services required to provide affluent clients with retirement advice and investment management. We assist clients in developing a detailed understanding of what their financial needs and objectives are, and then develop a plan whereby each client is assured of achieving these objectives. The company is a Registered Investment Advisor (RIA) with the Securities and Exchange Commission, providing individual clients with financial plan development, financial advisory, and money management services.

Demographic trends are very favorable for AFG. The affluent market has consistently been a very profitable market for financial service providers. The number of wealthy individuals in search of financial advisory services and investment advisory services is growing rapidly. The outlook for wealth accumulation is good; the U.S. economy has become more competitive globally, increasing the opportunity for the wealthy to increase their assets. There has also been a boom in the number of new small business owners over the past decade, and the trend for new business development is accelerating as talented executives and managers have been downsized out of larger companies. Seniors in America are the wealthiest generation on record and require retirement advice and investment services to manage their wealth. Baby boomers are entering their peak earning and savings years and will require more help with their financial decision making as they accumulate wealth and approach retirement.

The investment management business is growing. More and more, affluent investors are searching for high-quality professional investment management. Some independent advisors are meeting this challenge by creating their own boutique investment management programs. However, like us, the vast majority of advisors are outsourcing portfolio management of their affluent clients' assets to companies providing turnkey asset management programs or wrap programs. This leaves the investment advisor the time necessary to be more keenly focused on the selling and relationship management aspects involved in working successfully in the affluent client market. Supporting this trend is the dynamic shift across the financial services marketplace to gather assets in a fee-based convention to create a recurring revenue stream for the advisor and the firms they are affiliated with.

Strategic Opportunities

AFG's reputation as a trusted advisor with the demonstrated ability to provide corporate human resources departments, retiring executives, and affluent seniors with the highest quality retirement planning advice and investment management service should be able to consistently attract new clients, allowing for continued expansion and growth of the firm.

TARGET MARKET ANALYSIS

Affluent investors are noted for being less price and performance sensitive than either retail or institutional investors. Financial and investment management for the affluent is a relationship business. The high-net-worth client wants to develop a face-to-face interpersonal relationship with an advisor who can provide turnkey financial management, problem solving, and peace of mind. The financial services industry catering to the affluent investor is fairly fragmented and competitive. Because this is a highly profitable area, it has drawn many industry competitors.

AFG's ideal target client is 45 to 70 years old, has a net worth of $1,000,000 or more with at least $500,000 of assets to invest, and needs retirement planning services.

A Fragmented Industry

The investment management and advisory business focused on the affluent is highly fragmented; no one advisor appears to have more than 1 percent of the two million liquid millionaires in the United States. Over the near term, Anne sees unlimited opportunity to attract more clients. However, the success of the financial planner/investment advisor in working with the affluent will likely draw additional competition from financial institutions such as banks and brokerage and insurance companies, who are all looking to carve up a piece of the affluent market by offering financial planning services. This competitive onslaught may well cause consolidation of our fragmented industry, which will centralize market share to a hundred or so large institutions. This consolidation phase should provide a good backdrop for Anne to exit the business over the next five years, should she decide to sell.

Demographic Trends

There are 35,000,000 seniors in America, who have an estimated $14 trillion in total net worth, $7 trillion of which is investable assets. As they pass their assets to the next generation, their entire asset base will become liquid, significantly increasing the amount of investable assets that will need to be managed by the next generation. The 76,000,000 baby boomers in America have an estimated $3 trillion in retirement plan assets. Boomers are entering their peak earning and savings years, and need more help making financial decisions as they accumulate, inherit, and approach retirement.

While there are tremendous demographic changes driving demand for financial planning services, there are estimated to be only 20,000 financial planners in the United States providing clients with the high level of financial planning advice and turnkey financial management. The dynamics of an aging population, combined with increasing wealth, provide significant growth opportunities for AFG.

AFG is working to expand market opportunities by developing an institutional service platform to allow for growth of its client base while maintaining the ability to deliver a superior level of advice and service. The company plans to mine existing client relationships for new referrals to allow associate planners to quickly grow the practice. AFG recognizes that competition is increasing as many new entrants—such as CPAs, attorneys, and brokers—vie for clients, and recognizes the need to continue to acquire new client relationships over the near term to increase the size of the business.

THE COMPETITION

One could be easily overwhelmed by the number of institutional competitors targeting the affluent market, but the competitive advantages favor AFG because of the trust and strong interpersonal relationships the company develops with affluent clients. In addition, AFG currently offers clients a more robust offering of high-quality, value-added financial advisory services than its competition. As a matter of fact, industry competitors view the independent investment advisory firms with their demonstrated ability to build and nurture the client relationship as their most competitive threat. (3=Highest, 2=Moderate, 1=Low) Prince, R.A. & File, K.M., *Building Your Success: Competitor Perceptions by Competitor*, HNW Press, 1997.

Competitors	Entrepreneurial	Technical Savvy	People Focused
Independent RIAs	3	3	3
Private Banks	1	1	3
Brokers	2	2	2
Family Offices	1	3	2
Mutual Fund Cos.	2	3	2
Insurance Agents	3	2	3

As larger, well-capitalized competitors enter the affluent market to provide financial planning and turnkey management, there will be greater price pressure and commoditization of service, which will bring profits of smaller independent planners under pressure. The Internet will become a communication medium that will revolutionize the financial business. The proliferation of financial information available on the Internet will cause the perception that financial information alone will have little inherent value. Clients will continue to focus on building a relationship with an advisor capable of global problem solving and management. One of the societal trends that will ensure that the vast majority of seniors and boomers will continue to seek out advice and management is their need to develop an increased quality of life as they mature. As their affluence and account size grow, few will opt to risk their financial well-being by becoming their own part-time financial managers over the Internet.

Competitive Analysis: How Do Clients Perceive Your Advice and Service

Category Rank 1–10 (1=Low, 10=High)	Your Firm	Other Local Financial Planners	CPA Firms	Brokers	Banks
Service Menu and Benefits	10	8	7	6	5
Service Cost	6	7	4	5	8
Implementation Cost	9	7	6	5	3
Value-Added Savings	9	8	8	5	4
Quality of Advice and Service	9	8	8	5	6
Perceived Value of Advice and Service	10	8	7	5	6
Image	7	6	6	8	9
Name Recognition	5	3	5	10	9
Customer Relationships- Trust	10	9	8	6	6
Office Location	7	6	7	9	10
Delivery Time	8	6	5	3	4
Convenience of Use	10	9	7	6	10
Credit Policies	5	6	6	9	9
Customer Service	10	8	7	7	7
Social Image	8	7	8	7	10
Other: _____					
Total Points	123	106	99	96	106

Competitive Analysis: How Do You Rank Your Firm Against Competitors?

Category Rank 1–10 (1=Low, 10=High)	Your Firm	Other Financial Planners	CPA Firms	Brokers	Banks
Financial Resources	5	3	6	10	9
Marketing Program	5	4	3	10	8
Technological Competence	9	6	4	8	5
Access to Distribution	4	3	2	10	9
Access to Other Professionals	5	3	5	10	9
Economies of Scale	3	1	4	10	9
Operational Efficiencies	8	5	4	8	5
Sales Process/ Competence	10	8	5	7	3
Consulting Menu Breadth	9	6	6	7	5
Strategic Partnerships	5	3	4	10	7
Company Personnel	8	6	7	7	5
Knowledge Level	10	8	8	5	3
Certification/ Regulatory	8	6	4	9	5
Patents/Trademarks	5	1	1	7	5
Industry Contacts	5	4	4	10	8
Other:					
Total Points	99	67	67	128	95

AFG's reputation, size, and the quality of service give it a competitive advantage over many individual consultants. AFG's understanding of the affluent client's needs, combined with an understanding of the effective business model required to deliver these services, will allow AFG to focus the company's resources more effectively than our competitors. Our focus on retirement planning provides us with a niche opportunity to continue to be highly specialized.

PRODUCTS AND SERVICES

AFG's target market for its products and services is the affluent executive or senior approaching retirement who wants professional advice and management to achieve retirement goals.

AFG has defined our planning clients to have a minimum net worth of $1,000,000, with investable assets of at least $250,000. The ideal client would have a net worth of at least $1,000,000 and investable assets of at least $500,000. Because the planning business is dependent on effectively managing client relationships, the number of client relationships that can be successfully managed limits business growth.

Our services are based on a comprehensive analysis delivered through a traditional financial plan. We then provide clients with a broad spectrum of investment and insurance products to meet their needs. We traditionally use a combination of load funds—variable annuities, fee-based mutual fund allocation, and individual security wrap-fee programs—to implement client investment programs. Insurance is focused on estate planning and long-term-care requirements.

Our service focus is to provide clients with retirement planning solutions and investment management services that enable them to achieve their retirement goals. We plan to broaden our planning approach to include other services such as estate planning, cash flow planning, and income tax planning, which our client's continue to request.

Transition to Fee-Based Planning and Assets Management

AFG's plan to convert existing client positions in load mutual funds to fee-based management will require the company to provide a higher level of client education and service. The company plans to offer a standardized service plan to clients who transition to the fee-based model. Central to the new service plan will be continuous updates to each client's financial plan. AFG plans to offer updates as each client transitions to fee-based investment management programs and then annually thereafter. AFG also wants to make sure it not only responds to client needs but initiates proactive client contact to strengthen its relationship with each client. To that end AFG has developed a minimum service profile for each client so every employee knows exactly what service needs to be provided to each client.

AFG Client Service Program

Standard Planning Client Profile	Minimum	Service Provided	Frequency
Income	$ 100,000	Comprehensive Financial Plan	Annually
Net Worth	$1,000,000	Implementation Service	Ongoing
Total Investment Assets	$ 500,000	Investment Reports	Quarterly
Fee-Based Managed Assets	$ 250,000	In-person Investment Review	Annually
		Tax Review	Annually
Premier Planning Client Profile	Minimum	Service Provided	Frequency
Income	$ 100,000	Comprehensive Financial Plan	Annually
Net Worth	$2,000,000	Implementation Service	Ongoing
Total Investment Assets	$1,000,000	Investment Reports	Quarterly
Fee-Based Managed Assets	$ 750,000	In-person Investment Review	Semi-annually
		Tax Review	Semi-annually

MARKETING PLAN AND SALES STRATEGY

AFG's marketing plan is to leverage its unique position as a leading provider of retirement-focused financial planning services to affluent clients by communicating a clear message of the value in working with AFG.

AFG's reputation for delivering the highest quality planning and advisory services has placed us in the enviable position of receiving more qualified referrals from our existing clients than we can currently handle. AFG routinely provides corporate resource departments with seminars, which are extremely well received by employees. These corporate-sponsored seminars provide the company with more referred prospects than can be currently handled without increased sales staff. We have instituted a plan to hire and train associate planners to allow AFG to significantly increase sales and broaden the sales effort beyond Anne as the key sales producer.

OPERATIONS

At the core of AFG's strategic plan is the need to institutionalize corporate operations and the management of the company. To this end the company has continued its practices and procedures designing standard operating procedures, which will enable employees to handle work more efficiently. New sales and staff training programs will also enable AFG to train associate planners, as well as practice administrators to increase the company's ability to continue to grow while providing the quality of advice and service necessary to maintain our reputation. Our service commitment throughout the organization is to provide a very high level of service that our clients require and our competitors will find hard to duplicate.

Most financial salespeople chase the up-front revenue associated with making the affluent prospect a client. Our operational focus is to provide a very high level of service, ensuring happy clients and high fee-based revenue retention. To highlight how important client revenue retention is, we need only to look at the revenue generated by our average client: Our average client with a million dollar net worth and $500,000 to invest generates first year revenue of *$15,000,* but average revenue increases over time due to asset growth averaging approximately *$13,000* per year over 10 years and *$18,000* over 20 years. Creating a high level of recurring revenue is critical to accomplishing our strategic goal, and by converting existing load-based funds to fee-based management, while gathering new client assets in fee-based programs, we will meet our goal of increasing the equity value of our organization.

STRATEGIC GOALS AND MILESTONES

Strategic Objective

Our strategic objective is to change our sales practice into an institutional quality financial planning company providing financial advice, service, and investment management, which will help clients retire comfortably. It is to also broaden the management structure of the organization providing for corporate continuity for clients and employees, while increasing the inherent value of the company.

AFG's organizational goals include:

- Implement and effectively communicate the company's mission statement, corporate philosophy, strategic objective, and strategic plan to employees.
- Establish an equity-sharing plan to attract and retain new key employees, providing them with an incentive to aggressively achieve the strategic goals of the company.
- Develop an employee appraisal and performance system, which will tie employee compensation to strategic goal achievement.
- Institutionalize management processes and service delivery so that all clients perceive value in maintaining a relationship with the company, not the individual planner.

- Develop a sales and training program for new financial planners.
- Develop a training program for VP of Operations.
- Develop a detailed job description for each employee and have each employee develop a set of standard operating procedures covering all aspects of his or her job.

AFG's sales and revenue goals include:

- Limit the number of new clients to those with $500,000 or more to invest.
- Provide comprehensive planning services to new and existing clients.
- Allocate 50 percent of new assets gathered to fee-based programs.
- Convert $15,000,000 of commission-based assets held by existing clients to fee-based management programs each year.
- Transition Anne's rainmaker status to new planners over the next three years, allowing her to work part-time.
- Target 50 percent income from recurring streams within three years.

Milestone and Goal Planning

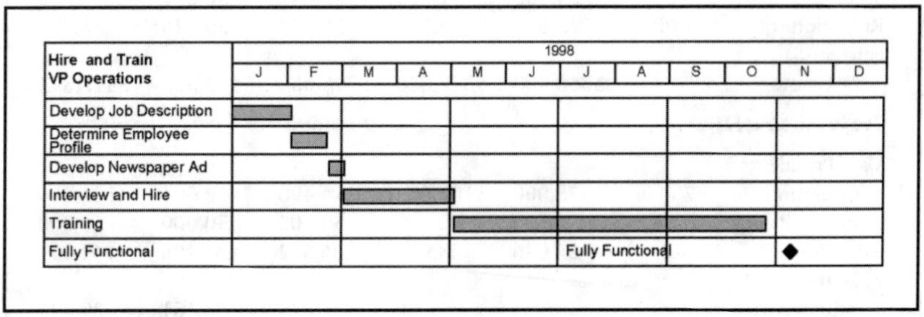
Hire and Train VP Operations
1998
J
F
M
A
M
J
J
A
S
O
N
D
Develop Job Description
Determine Employee Profile
Develop Newspaper Ad
Interview and Hire
Training
Fully Functional
Fully Functional

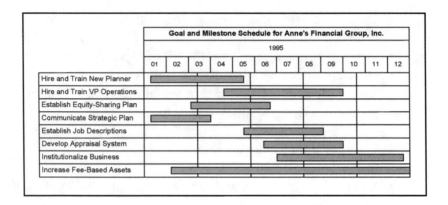

FINANCIAL PROJECTIONS

Salary Overhead Planning Model

		Employees				
Title	Growth Factor	Salary 1998	Salary 1999	Salary 2000	Salary 2001	Salary 2002
President— Anne	0.00%	$200,000	$200,000	$200,000	$200,000	$200,000
Planning Manager	7.00	50,000	53,500	57,245	61,252	65,540
Bookkeeper	7.00	33,000	35,310	37,782	40,426	43,256
Planning Administrator	7.00	30,000	32,100	34,347	36,751	39,324
Secretary	7.00	28,000	29,960	32,057	34,301	36,702
Receptionist	7.00	25,000	26,750	28,623	30,626	32,770
Current Salary Overhead		$366,000	$377,620	$390,053	$403,357	$417,592
Projected New Hires:				9 Months		
Vice-President Operations	7.00%	$75,000	$107,000	$114,490	$122,504	$131,080
Associate Planner	0.00	37,500	50,000	50,000	50,000	50,000
Sales Bonus		27,086	88,919	106,332	123,995	142,499
Planning Administrator	7.00	0	0	34,347	36,751	39,324
Projected New Salaries		$139,586	$245,919	$305,169	$333,251	$362,902
Total Projected Salaries		$505,586	$623,539	$695,223	$736,608	$780,494

Anne's Profit and Loss Statement

Year	1998	1999	2000	2001	2002
Total Revenue	$934,720	$991,679	$1,122,383	$1,252,484	$1,450,962
Total Expenses	$673,166	$808,705	$ 892,444	$ 942,299	$ 995,066
Profit (Loss)	$261,554	$182,974	$ 229,939	$ 310,185	$ 455,897

Anne's Revenue Projections

Assumptions:

Average Annual Return on AUM	8.00%				
Average Asset Management Fee	0.85%				
Average Client Assets Invested	$ 500,000				
Average Planning Fee	$500				
Average Commission on Funds	4.00%				
Net Equity Trail	0.25%				
Existing Fee-Based Assets	$15,000,000				
Existing Commission Based Assets	$45,000,000				
% of New Assets Committed to Fee	50.00%				
Conversion Rate Comm. to Fee	50.00%				
Average Insurance Comm./Client	$ 1,500				

Sales Projections:	1998	1999	2000	2001	2002
New Clients Anne	30	15	10	5	5
New Clients Associate Planner	10	20	20	20	20
New Assets Anne	$15,000,000	$ 7,500,000	$ 5,000,000	$ 2,500,000	$ 2,500,000
New Assets Associate Planner	$ 5,000,000	$10,000,000	$10,000,000	$10,000,000	$10,000,000
Total New Assets	$20,000,000	$17,500,000	$15,000,000	$12,500,000	$12,500,000
Conversion of Comm. Assets to Fee	$ 7,500,000	$ 7,500,000	$ 7,500,000	$ 7,500,000	$ 7,500,000
New Assets Committed to Fee	$10,000,000	$ 8,750,000	$ 7,500,000	$ 6,250,000	$ 6,250,000
Total New Fee-Based Assets	$17,500,000	$16,250,000	$15,000,000	$13,750,000	$13,750,000

Revenue Projections:	1998	1999	2000	2001	2002
Planning Fees	$ 20,000	$ 17,500	$ 15,000	$ 12,500	$ 12,500
Equity Commissions	$ 400,000	$ 350,000	$ 300,000	$ 250,000	$ 250,000
Equity Trails	$ 128,000	$ 141,490	$ 152,809	$ 161,784	$ 171,477
Insurance Commissions	$ 60,000	$ 52,500	$ 45,000	$ 37,500	$ 37,500
Insurance Renewals	$ 35,000	$ 41,000	$ 46,250	$ 50,750	$ 54,500
AUM Fee-Based Revenue	$ 291,720	$ 389,189	$ 563,324	$ 739,950	$ 924,986
Total Revenue	$ 934,720	$ 991,679	$ 1,122,383	$ 1,252,484	$ 1,450,962
Percentage of Recurring Revenue	50.79%	59.41%	69.26%	77.05%	80.19%

Anne's Expense Model

EXPENSES	Growth Factor	1998	1999	2000	2001	2002
Salary Overhead		$505,586	$623,539	$695,223	$736,608	$780,494
Payroll Taxes 6.17%		31,195	38,472	42,895	45,449	48,156
Benefits @ 6%		30,335	37,412	41,713	44,196	46,830
Printing and						
Repro	5.00%	2,500	2,625	2,756	2,894	3,039
Rent	3.00	24,000	24,720	25,462	26,225	27,012
Travel and						
Entertainment	3.00	2,500	2,575	2,652	2,732	2,814
Telephone	3.00	6,000	6,180	6,365	6,556	6,753
Conference						
Expenses	3.00	2,000	2,060	2,122	2,185	2,251
Advertising	3.00	1,500	1,545	1,591	1,639	1,688
Professional Fees	3.00	4,000	4,120	4,244	4,371	4,502
Software Updates	3.00	2,500	2,575	2,652	2,732	2,814
Cleaning	3.00	1,500	1,545	1,591	1,639	1,688
Dues and Fees	3.00	800	824	849	874	900
Contributions	3.00	250	258	265	273	281
Misc. Expenses	3.00	1,000	1,030	1,061	1,093	1,126
Utilities	3.00	2,400	2,472	2,546	2,623	2,701
Licensing Fees	3.00	1,400	1,442	1,485	1,530	1,576
Bank Charge	3.00	200	206	212	219	225
Computer						
Consultants	3.00	8,000	8,240	8,487	8,742	9,004
Postage and						
Delivery	3.00	2,800	2,884	2,971	3,060	3,151
Auto Expense	3.00	2,200	2,266	2,334	2,404	2,476
Auto Lease	3.00	6,000	6,180	6,365	6,556	6,753
Insurance						
Expenses	3.00	3,000	3,090	3,183	3,278	3,377
Equipment						
Leases	3.00	18,000	18,540	19,096	19,669	20,259
Leasehold						
Improvements	3.00	1,200	1,236	1,273	1,311	1,351
Employee						
Benefit Plan c	3.00	800	824	849	874	900
Petty Cash	3.00	500	515	530	546	563
Office Supplies	3.00	11,000	11,330	11,670	12,020	12,381
Total		**$673,166**	**$808,705**	**$892,444**	**$942,299**	**$995,066**

RESOURCE ANALYSIS

Human Resources Analysis

Over the past several years we have identified the need to institutionalize the management of our human resources. We have recognized the need to implement a companywide confidentiality program to ensure client information is kept in the strictest confidence. We also need to develop a job description program, salary administration program, and standardized annual employee review process. In addition, we will need to initiate the following:

- Develop and implement a noncompete program for executives and associate planners.
- Develop an equity-sharing plan to compensate and retain valuable employees.
- Hire a vice-president to run corporate operations and to coordinate planning activities.
- Hire an associate planner to broaden the company's sales capacity.
- Develop training programs for new hires.

Resource Partners

To effectively implement our strategic business plan we need to enlist the help of all resource partners. The company has communicated its strategic plan with several key partners who will bring their resources to bear in helping the company implement its strategy. First, our NASD broker-dealer has offered to use its recruiting department to locate a suitable associate planner and management candidate for the VP of Operations position. In addition, they have offered financial incentives to help offset the fixed costs of training new salespeople until they become productive. Second, the company's CPA firm has offered to increase qualified affluent client referrals if AFG shares case revenue with them. This will allow

Anne more time to train new employees rather than spending her time marketing.

Financial Resources

A key part of AFG's strategic plan is a financial analysis to determine if the company has the financial resources to implement the plan. As CEO, Anne is particularly concerned about the new fixed overhead she will be forced to assume by expanding her employee base. She projects AFG will incur approximately $150,000 of new salary overhead over the next 18 months. Projections indicate that she will be able to cover these expenses initially by reinvesting the firm's profit, which will reduce her take home pay. Because cash flow management is critical to business success, it is obvious to Anne that AFG needs to accelerate conversion of load funds to fee-based programs. This will not only increase revenue, but will also provide more predictable cash flow to support increased overhead.

CRITICAL RISKS

Regulatory

The pace of regulatory change is a constant challenge to AFG. Some regulatory change, like the 1996 changes to the Investment Advisors Act providing for a two tier investment advisor registration, has increased the barriers to competition. The SEC will now only supervise RIAs who have in excess of $25,000,000 under management. Smaller advisors must register with each state to do business. There is a perceived competitive disadvantage to not being large enough to be a SEC registered advisor. However, AFG should have enough assets under management by year-end 1999 to register with the SEC.

Unfortunately, the pace of regulatory change disrupts human resource allocation and strains cash flow to keep pace with the level of change. To alleviate this strain, AFG has outsourced its regulatory compliance to a nationally recognized firm specializing in RIA compliance.

Lack of Capital

Significant growth requires access to capital by leveraging existing cash flow through borrowing. The greatest risk to not accomplishing our strategic goals is the lack of adequate capital. Borrowing subjects the company to additional cash flow risk associated with timely loan repayment.

Lack of Management Experience

Anne is a great planner, but she is not a professional manager or experienced business builder. She may lack the experience required to delegate effectively and to focus on attaining business goals.

APPENDIX AND VALUATION

Management Team

Anne May, CFP, is Founder, President, and CEO of AFG, Inc., in Small Town, USA. She is a Certified Financial Planner (CFP) and member of the ICFP and the IAFP. She currently holds the following NASD licenses: Series 24, 7, 63, and 65. In 1996, Anne founded AFG, a financial planning firm. Anne has been extensively involved in the brokerage and financial planning industry since 1986. She is considered an expert on retirement planning issues and is often quoted in the press. In addition, she is a retirement planning consultant to several Fortune 500 companies. Anne received a bachelor's degree in Finance from the University of Maryland in 1985.

AFG's plans to increase sales capacity and institutionalize client relationships will cause the company to significantly expand

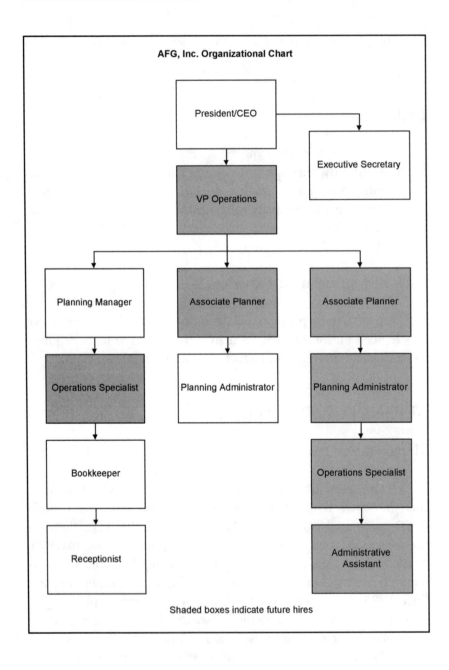

its employee base over the next few years. Critical initial hires are an associate planner to increase sales capacity and client service and a VP of Operations to take over key management functions.

Valuation

Establishing a valuation methodology is important to measuring the value of the company, the performance of management, and the contribution of employees, which determines performance-based equity compensation. AFG believes that its stock will be valuable in the near future and wants to make sure that it has a methodology for measuring the value being created by implementing its strategic plan.

Anne and her strategic planning coach have determined that AFG has already started converting their commission-based sales practice into a fee-based sales practice. The strategic plan she has developed will help AFG convert its sales practice to a fee-based business by converting the remaining load based funds to fee programs, and as new sales employees become fully trained, AFG will be able to institutionalize Anne's existing client relationships, increasing the value of the company and positioning the business for sale within Anne's targeted time frame.

Business Profile	Commission-Based Sales Practice	Fee-Based Sales Practice	Fee-Based Business
Existing Assets Invested in Load Funds	$60,000,000	$41,250,000	$41,250,000
New Money Invested in Load Product	$10,000,000	$10,000,000	$10,000,000
Existing Assets Under Fee Management	$ 0	$15,000,000	$15,000,000
New Assets Under Management	$ 0	$13,750,000	$17,500,000
Overhead Expense Factor (% of Gross Income)	46.00%	55.00%	55.00%
Retention Assumptions			
Financial Planning Fees	25.00%	25.00%	85.00%
Equity Commissions	12.50%	12.50%	50.00%
Equity Trails	25.00%	25.00%	50.00%
Asset Management Fees	50.00%	50.00%	85.00%
Group Compensation	50.00%	50.00%	85.00%
Insurance Commissions	0.00%	0.00%	25.00%
Value	$ 311,077	$ 616,920	$ 1,465,071

Technology and Workflow Solutions

TECHNOLOGY, TECHNOLOGY, AND TECHNOLOGY

Every major financial institution today is searching for a way to tap into the affluent investor marketplace. If you are an independent financial planner/investment advisor, you have to be wondering how you will compete and survive—much less continue to prosper and grow—in the coming turf war for the affluent client. And, make no mistake about it, it will be all out war!

Our conglomerate-sized competitors are definitely here to stay. They have the strategic focus and capital to make sure they get their fair share of the affluent marketplace; and if you're not careful, they'll take yours, too. Industry observers say we will have to compete on price with the conglomerates; otherwise, our revenue and margins will decline and our businesses will fail. They say this is a competitive battle that we cannot win, because the "big boys" have size, scale, and volume that we cannot hope to duplicate. Unfortunately, this could be true if you allow your business to compete this way.

However, our competitors' current dilemma is how to provide the same high-quality, client-specific financial advice, service, and turnkey financial management that affluent clients demand and that the independent advisor already provides. We should not lose sight of some very distinct advantages we have in this marketplace. Remember, the affluent client wants to develop a face-to-face interpersonal relationship with a trusted financial advisor, not a faceless conglomerate.

As independent advisors and planners, we have been providing the affluent with comprehensive financial planning services and the investment products they need to implement their plans for the past 20 to 30 years. Because we are independent, we can provide unbiased advice and the most appropriate product to solve their problems. Our ongoing service and consistent management ensures they ultimately achieve their goals.

So how do we level the playing field with the big boys? The answer to this question seems crystal clear: *Leverage your use of technology.*

Just as *location, location, location* is the essential ingredient to being successful with real estate, if you have developed your business plan and strategy, all you need to focus on to be successful in this new competitive environment is *technology, technology, technology.* Technology can empower your organization by providing access to meaningful information and solutions. It can enhance productivity, increasing your ability to grow revenue and profits, while providing clients with a level of advice and service that cannot be duplicated by competitors.

Don't compete! Set yourself and your organization *apart* from the competition by setting new standards for products and service. Develop technology solutions that streamline your workflow processes, reducing your reliance on people to push paper, which will increase efficiency and profit.

Our firm has invested significant resources to streamline our business model, creating standardized processes and procedures that can be automated and perfected through technology, and allowing us to provide clients with astounding service. Our technology strategy is to develop an end-to-end, enterprisewide technology platform that seamlessly integrates all of the front office, middle office, and back office functions of our business. (We must have more than a few business engineer personality types in our firm.)

FRONT OFFICE SOLUTIONS

For the past 20 to 30 years, the financial services industry has focused almost exclusively on client acquisition, making the initial sale. Due to the dynamic changes in consumer preferences—a desire to work with an advisor, not a product salesperson—we have seen a shift from up-front, commission-based compensation systems to ongoing fee-based systems. All this has caused an industrywide change in the myopic focus on making the initial sale to a more holistic focus on ongoing service leading to high client retention. Under the fee-based model, it is actually more important to retain existing clients and the commensurate increasing revenue stream than to acquire new ones. As an industry, we need to radically re-engineer existing sales practice models to an institutional business model that focuses on developing technology solutions to ensure top-quality ongoing service and financial management. Obviously, new client acquisition is important to the growth and survival of any business, but in a fee-based business you can't afford to lose existing clients due to poor service while pursuing new clients.

New Sales Systems Required

In the past, most of the sales focus has been on the activities required to acquire clients, principally *prospect conversion and ethical persuasion*. To meet the demands of servicing and retaining clients, you must develop new programs centered around *ongoing client education and relationship management*. You can use a uniform sales process to constantly reinforce your relationship as advisors with clients and educate them on the benefits of having you manage their investments.

Here's how we institutionalized our sales process, understanding that client retention is still a function of sales.

Stage I is prospect conversion:

- *Building blocks introduction.* This part of our sales talk is
  specifically designed to provide prospects with an introduction to our financial planning process, mission statement,
  and corporate philosophy. The introduction provides the
  prospect with general information about the financial planning process while illustrating the financial problems people
  encounter without the benefit of comprehensive planning.
- *Sweat tracks.* In this phase of our sales talk we interview the
  client to gain an understanding of the client's situation, allowing the planner to evaluate and point out the client's
  current financial problems while demonstrating the benefit
  of working with our firm to solve these problems. There
  are two sweat track levels—the building blocks sweat track,
  which is basic and used in all client interview situations, and
  the estate planning sweat track, more advanced and used
  with more affluent clients with complex financial situations.

Stage II is ethical persuasion:

- *Data-taking sweat track.* It is during the data-taking session
  that the planner has the opportunity to evaluate the prospect's situation to determine specific problems and offer
  potential solutions. This sweat track is a process that arms
  the planner with the sweat questions necessary to make the
  client uncomfortable enough to motivate the client to make
  the necessary changes to solve those problems. Any sales
  that are eventually made to the client are discussed during
  this phase, which makes the plan presentation and implementation meeting anticlimatic and void of controversy.
- *Plan presentation sales track.* Presenting a financial plan is
  not an art but a science. This sales track creates a presentation process that shows the clients a detailed picture of

where they are today and where they need to go to accomplish their objectives by concentrating on their current
problems and the recommended solutions. One of the problems solved by our plan presentation sales track is to reduce
the complexity and overwhelming quantity of information
delivered in the financial plan presentation to a format that
allows clients to understand their financial plan and the
changes they need to make to attain their objectives.

- *Implementation sales track.* Gaining effective implementation is also a science and needs to be reduced to a systematic
process to ensure high closing ratios and strict adherence to
compliance during the sales process.

Stage III is client education and relationship management,
which includes the investment sales track. A large portion of recurring revenue that we need to capture is generated from fees on investment assets under management. One of the largest risks to a
fee-based model is losing assets because of poor performance or
not living up to client expectations. These are particularly dangerous waters to navigate for advisors.

Managing client investment expectations is more science than
art. It requires the ability to focus client expectations on the ultimate investment outcome necessary to achieve their planning goals
(e.g., retirement funding or education funding). By helping clients
understand their required rate of return and defining the level of
risk they are willing to tolerate in pursuing this return, you can
manage their expectations to enable them to win as investors.

At WBI, we have spent the past 20 years working with affluent investors who come to us for investment advice and management when they are nearing or are in retirement. Over the years we
have identified certain common traits about investors who fit into
this category. They have spent a lifetime saving and accumulating
enough money to help them retire comfortably and almost without exception, these folks sit across the conference table and tell us
that this is all the money they have to live on, so don't lose it. They
tell us they don't have the time or desire to try to build another

nest egg. This has led us to develop an entire investment management process to "invest our clients serious money, the money they cannot afford to lose."

With the help of a competent planner, investors can determine their required rate of return (ROR). Once investors know their ROR, they then need to take a careful look at their attitudes about the risks. We spend a lot of time with clients to determine exactly what their investments need to accomplish for them before we make investment recommendations. Because we focus on our clients' serious money, we have found that investors' perception about risks in investing their money needs to be thoroughly investigated before making investment decisions. The combination of these factors should be recorded in the client investment policy statement, a written document that outlines the rules for making investment management decisions. Much has been written about evaluating investment risk tolerance, but the most critical factor, investor risk, is often overlooked.

In the process of building an investment strategy, a lot of time and attention is typically spent identifying, assessing, and addressing various investment risks. Just as dangerous to the ultimate success of an investment program, however, is the effect emotions can have on investor behavior. We refer to this as *investor risk*. In our opinion, investment policies that do not address this risk are deficient. So we developed an investment sales track and client education program to discuss the markets, return expectations, and risk inherent to investing. This sales track educates the client on the benefits of understanding what it takes to become successful as an investor. We hold client education meetings with most of our clients at least twice per year to reinforce these concepts and manage client investment expectations.

Tracking Sales and Revenue

I recently attended an industry conference with a breakout session on practice technology. Near the end of the session, the moderator asked the audience to describe areas where they need new technology solutions. One of the first people to respond was a successful planner who described how he had just discovered that he had not been paid trail commissions totaling $10,000 from a mutual fund company over the past year. He went on to say that he was concerned that this might be the "tip of the iceberg," that this might not be the only compensation that he had not been paid. He said he did not have a system to accurately keep track of revenue. Many other advisors rallied behind him to say that they have the same concerns.

Our sales tracker database module tracks expected revenue by client, planner, service provided, product sold, and business unit. Most planning practices use cash-basis financial reporting and standardized financial reporting software, and have no way of keeping track of expected revenue from planning activities.

Because financial planning is typically a long sales cycle, it is difficult for the planning firm to forecast revenue. As you grow and increase your fixed overhead, it is extremely important to know that you can cover your expenses over the near term, say over the next three to six months. Without a sales tracking system that captures expected revenue, you have no way of knowing if your business will be able to meet its expenses. A system needs to capture expected revenue and track it all the way through paid status. In our office, this system allows us to determine if we are on track to meet forecasts and acts as an early warning system to allow management to intervene to solve problems by stimulating sales or by cutting expenses.

Our sales tracker system also provides management with key sales performance reports to indicate planner's closing ratios, as well as service and relationship management productivity levels. Because it is a point-of-sale tracking system, we have also integrated regulatory compliance, tracking all sales activities to ensure licensing compliance for each product and service provided to clients in their state of residence. In addition, the information captured provides an electronic system to generate required compliance reports, such as a transaction blotter, cash and securities blotter, and prod-

uct concentration blotter. The same system and information provide the basis to track revenue and to pay commissions.

This sales tracking module provides:

- Tracking of expected revenue from new clients
  - By planner
  - By service
  - By product
  - By business unit
- Tracking of booked revenue-completed sales
  - By planner
  - By service
  - By product
  - By business unit
- Commission payment tracking
  - Commission due to company
  - Commission due to reps
  - Commission reporting and payment
- OSJ Blotter Compliance System

Sales tracking includes:

- Product input forms, including type, compensation, blotter
- Rep input forms, new reps
- Client selection query, select applicable client
- Expected income
  - Transaction number
  - Expected date
  - Expected transaction
  - Client name
  - Product code
  - Rep code
  - Expected gross comp
  - Expected split comp
- Booked income
  - Booked date (blotter) (investment tracking module)

- Booked transaction
- Booked gross comp
- Booked split comp
- Expected pay date
- Revenue forecasting and tracking
  - Recurring revenue
  - Expected revenue report
  - Booked revenue report
  - Expected pay date report (aging)
  - Exception report
  - Rep report, including product allocation charting

The NASD/OSJ compliance includes:

- Securities blotter
  - Trade amount
  - Trade date
  - Account number
  - Product
  - Confirmation number
  - Trader ID
- Checks and securities received log
  - Security name
  - Client name
  - Amount
  - Date received
  - Received via
  - Received by
  - Sent date
  - Sent to
  - Sent via

Licensing compliance includes:

- Licensing and registration
  - Jurisdictions

- License type
- Expiration date
- CE requirements
- Renewal instructions
- Continuing education
  - Credits earned
  - Earned via
  - Jurisdiction(s)

MIDDLE AND BACK OFFICE SOLUTIONS

The middle-office functions of a financial planning business need to center on client relationship management. The relationship management functions are the most important activities and will determine the long-term success of your business. The relationship part of the equation is absolutely the key to retaining affluent clients.

To program effective technology solutions that enhance work-flow in these areas, we need to develop uniform service modules for client service and management. Uniform service profiles empower all employees in your organization to successfully manage the client relationship and service needs, thereby enhancing timeliness of service delivery. This provides time for additional client acquisition while maintaining our commitment to provide clients with the highest levels of advice and service.

Lets take a look for a few minutes at what we imagine that this type of technology can do for you and your employees in your daily work lives: You get a message that one of your clients, Tom Jones, is holding for you on line 1. You toggle to your communications tracker portal and type Jones, then select Tom from the drop down list. You pick up the phone and greet Tom, and as you are discussing pleasantries, you review the most recent communications that Tom has had with your staff. You can see that, unbeknownst to you, Tom called in last week to request information on a mutual fund he recently read about. You note that your sales assistant has completed the task of sending out the prospectus and sales information.

You immediately ask Tom if he received the information on the mutual fund he requested and ask how you can help him today. He says that he received the information and can't believe how efficient your staff and company is in responding to his needs. But, he goes on to say, that the reason he is calling today is to discuss his desire to buy a new sports car for $65,000. He wants your opinion, as his advisor, if he can afford to make the purchase with cash and what will be the corresponding effect on his cash flow. After assuring Tom that you will take a look at his situation and call him back with answers to his questions, you record the conversation in the communications tracker.

From the same screen, you select the event tracker and write a detailed list of tasks for your planning manager to perform in order to answer your client's questions. You assign the task to your planning manager with a completion date and forward the task by e-mail as a message and directly to his personal task list. Your planning manager accepts the task and responds by e-mail that he will have the task completed within the allotted time frame. The next day, you receive e-mail notice that the task is complete with an attachment that shows the analysis and a customized form letter that provides the client with an overview. You briefly review the letter and analysis, confirming to your planning manager a job well done and instructions to forward the letter and analysis by e-mail and hard copy to your client, Tom. You then call Tom and discuss your recommendation with him. Your level of service once again astounds Tom and he provides you with two new referrals over the phone.

After hanging up with Tom, you enter the new referrals into your prospect tracker and initiate your automated process of converting these referral leads to clients. Your assistant is notified by e-mail of the new prospects received and she prints out the form referral letter and mails your marketing material. Your prospect tracker program sends you an e-mail notice and task to place a follow-up phone call five days from the time the letters went out. Time is valuable, but because of technology, you have been able to assign, coordinate, and complete multiple tasks in a matter of minutes. Sounds pretty good so far, doesn't it?

The single greatest challenge to providing comprehensive client-specific planning is effectively managing the myriad of details and tasks required to be completed on behalf of planning clients. To drive productivity and ensure fault tolerant service to clients, we have developed a database and workflow technology platform just like the example provided. As the software industry moves away from data warehousing technology to workflow enhancing technology, these types of tools will be available. This technology will provide planning organizations with not only data or detail management, but with the step-by-step procedures employees can follow for accomplishing complex service task sets. Our entire system has been designed to facilitate workflow efficiency while providing clients with effective implementation of financial planning recommendations.

As you analyze your business and begin to institutionalize your processes and procedures, you can also begin to develop solutions that supercharge your business.

These are the desired technology platform components:

- Data warehousing and management
- Financial planning presentation system
- Financial plan implementation and tracking
  - Financial plan manufacturing
  - Investment implementation
  - Insurance implementation
  - Estate planning and documentation development
- Service module
  - Tax reviews
  - Plan updates
  - Administration meetings
  - Investment reviews
  - Estate administration
- Client service platform implementation
  - Provides planner alerts prompting them to perform relationship management and service activities

- Tracks client service implementation
- Provides management reports and tracking of service provided
- Provides for employee and planner performance tracking
- Standard operating procedure integration
  - Provides procedures and instruction for complex service tasks
  - Single source for service procedures

Prospecting Module

This is the initial data entry point for a prospective client into our client management system. Data entry must include name, address, and telephone number, and the current client who referred them to us. It provides for custom correspondence to client, alerts to reps as to action items, appointments, etc., and alerts to planning staff regarding action items, such as contracting and initial data gathering.

Features include:

- Communication generation
  - Client specific
  - Planner/rep specific
  - Planning staff
- Action items tracking
  - Appointments
  - Correspondence
  - Initial data gathering
  - Contracting

Benefits include:

- Ensures fail-safe delivery of service platform. Every prospective client receives the same level of commitment from staff, to prove from the outset WBI is committed and able to provide them with the highest level of advice and service.

- Provides meaningful reporting to management identifying sales trends, clients in pipeline, planner/rep effectiveness, and planning staff effectiveness.

Planning Data-Tracking Module

This module guides staff through the process of collecting planning data from new clients. All appropriate correspondence and follow up is driven from this module.

Features include:

- Standard WBI Factfinder includes expense information, as well as risk tolerance section from confidential client questionnaire
- Identify required data
- Generate correspondence for requesting needed data
- Track request/receipt of data
- Prompt for written and/or telephone follow up for missing data
- Follow-up task assignment
- Provide instructions for input of data to FAST*planner* or financial planning software

Benefits include:

- Accurate financial plans can only be generated from accurate data.
- Timely and accurate data collection is crucial to accurate planning as well as short plan turnaround times.
- Short plan turnaround time improves cash flow planning as well as builds good will with clients as to timely service.

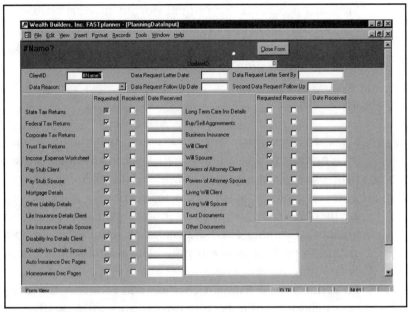

FASTPLANNER Planning Data Acquisition Details input form © WBI 1997

Financial Plan Development Module

This module creates client-specific financial plan recommendations from a standardized platform. All client plans follow the same process to ensure consistent final product across all planning areas. Data verification, analysis, and recommendation generation are handled in this area.

Features include:

- Data entry procedures designed to facilitate financial planning software usage
- Process tracking to identify bottlenecks
- Action steps according to procedure for completion of the planning process including data verification (upcurve), analysis of current situation, and client-specific recommendations
- Storage of previous data to generate cumulative benefit summary

- Standard procedure for printed document creation, binding, supporting documentation, etc.
- Standard procedures for appointment, conference room set-up, confirmation of appointments, etc.

Benefits include:

- Standard procedures for data entry, manipulation, and presentation facilitate lower staff level involvement rather than senior staff involvement. Standard planning analysis generation ensures consistency for client year to year (they are used to seeing their information presented in a uniform manner). Planning analysis generation standardized across clients to provide uniform presentation of financial plans, easing training process.
- Procedures for document creation and room set-up facilitates delegation of important tasks to appropriate staff level.

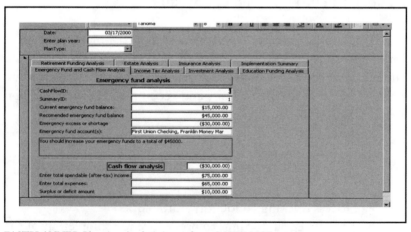

FASTPLANNER Planning Analysis input form © WBI 1997

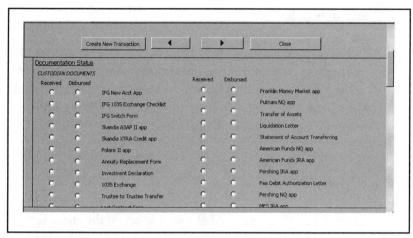

FASTPLANNER Account Processing input form © WBI 1997

Implementation Module

This module guides staff level employees through the process of implementing the various recommendations made in the financial plan including investments, insurance, estate planning, and other recommended strategies.

Features include:

- Investment tracking, including transaction blotter, cash flow tracking, follow-up triggers
- Insurance implementation section including documentation tracking, requirements tracking, follow-up triggers
- Estate planning section includes complete will preparation checklist, including provisions to be included, generating correspondence to attorney

Benefits include:

- All recommendations are captured for follow up. Implementation proceeds in a consistent manner while being monitored constantly. Ensures all items are completed as promised to client. Monitor for correct asset transfers including amounts, destinations, and compensation.

Service Module

This module will ensure the fail-safe delivery of the client service platform, including tax reviews, financial plan updates, investment reviews, plan administration meetings, trust administration, and other services as required. The service module empowers staff employees to complete tasks in timely fashion according to procedure.
Features include:

- Financial plan update module
- Communication-tracking module
- Tax review module
- Trust administration module
- Event-tracking module

Benefits include:

- Client service promises are kept without failure. Financial plan updates are initiated routinely at a predetermined start date. Client communication is also captured for follow up and compliance purposes. Tax review and reporting to accountants happen as matter of procedure rather than client request.
- Trust administration module ensures timely compliance with Crummey requirements and premium dates.
- All extraneous services are captured in the event tracker for follow up and completion.

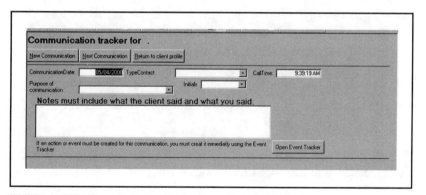

FASTPLANNER Update Checklist input form © WBI 1997

FASTPLANNER Communication Tracker input form © WBI 1997

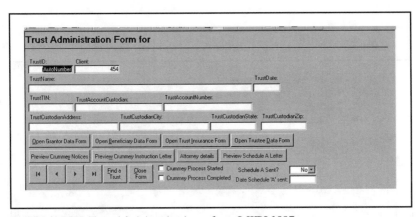

FASTPLANNER Event Tracker input form © WBI 1997

FASTPLANNER Trust Administration input form © WBI 1997

I N D E X